Christians, Wake Up!

J. J. Turner, PhD

Publishing Designs, Inc.
Huntsville, Alabama

Publishing Designs, Inc.
P.O. Box 3241
Huntsville, Alabama 35810

Printed in the United States of America

Publisher's Cataloging-in-Publication Data

Christians, wake up! / J. J. Turner
ISBN 978-0-929540-82-5
1. Christian mission. 2. Spiritual maturity 3. Biblical instruction
I. Title
253

To

James Andrews,

my friend, publisher, and fellow-worker

in the kingdom of God's dear Son.

Thanks, my brother,

for your encouragement and help.

—1 Corinthians 15:58

Contents

Preface

A number of readers of my other church leadership "wake up" books have asked, "When are you going to write one on wake up, Christians?" Well, here it is. This fourth volume in the wake-up series is *Christians, Wake Up!*

This fourth book is for every Christian. It is a wake-up call for God's army to stay awake and alert because of the challenges facing the church, both locally and universally. It has never been this late.

For some I imagine this book will be a wake-up call, a fresh breeze in the face of concern about the direction of the church, for others it will not be so refreshing; it will be tough and stuffy. In some circles it is not popular to talk about our issues; it is easier to keep one's head buried in the sand, hoping the challenges will go away. "Error circles the earth while truth puts its boots on."

It is never popular to summon people from a slumber or snooze; it is never popular to advocate an escape from the comfort zone of status quo. Yet this is what many Christians need—*a wake-up call!* A casting off of indifference and reengagement in our mission to preach the gospel to the entire world (Mark 16:15–16).

The world can see the love and righteousness of God only through the church, as it is reflected in the lives of members. The world is still requesting, "Sir, we would see Jesus." We have been called to be light, cities on a hill, salt, and leaven. Why? So we can be noticed, heard, and tasted. Christians must wake up to their mission in a lost and dying world.

If you are reading this, you are probably holding this book in your hands. A casual reading, which is commendable, will be of little benefit. Its message must be studied, prayed about, discussed, wrestled with, and applied. It is a personal wake-up call for the family of God, my family. Hopefully, it is a clarion voice crying in the spirit of the prophets to wake up and turn to the Lord with all our minds, hearts, souls, and strength. We need fresh fire (Jeremiah 20:9).

My prayer is that God will use this imperfect effort not only to wake me up but also to wake up my brothers and sisters—*you!*

J. J. Turner, PhD
September 9, 2011

Introduction

Wake-Up Calls for Some Christians

The apostle Paul challenged the Christians in Rome to wake up:

> And do this, knowing the time, that now it is high time to awake out of sleep; for now our salvation is nearer than when we first believed. The night is far spent, the day is at hand. Therefore let us cast off the works of darkness, and let us put on the armor of light (Romans 13:11–12).

Paul challenged the Christians at Corinth to wake up: "Awake to righteousness, and do not sin; for some do not have the knowledge of God. I speak this to your shame" (1 Corinthians 15:34).

Quoting from Isaiah 26:19 and 60:1, Paul wrote an application to the Christians at Ephesus:

> Therefore He says: "Awake, you who sleep, arise from the dead, and Christ will give you light." See that you walk circumspectly, not as fools but as wise, redeeming the time, because the day are evil (Ephesians 5:14–16).

From these and other verses we can conclude that identifying the need for a wake-up call is biblical. In my years of ministry I have noted numerous reasons that some Christians need wake-up calls. While it is true that not every Christian needs a wake-up call, sadly, many do.

What follows is a brief listening of areas in which some Christians need a wake-up call. As you read this list take a few minutes to do a self-awareness application. On a scale from 1 to 5, with 1 being sound asleep and 5 being fully awake, write where you feel you are on the scale:

1—Sound asleep
2—Dozing off
3—Catnapping
4—Drowsy
5—Wide awake

Some Christians need a wake-up call

____ from being lukewarm (Revelation 3:14–17)

____ from being carnally minded (1 Corinthians 3:1–4)

____ from being close-minded (Acts 17:11)

____ from walking by sight (2 Corinthians 5:7)

____ from neglecting prayer (1 Thessalonians 5:17)

____ from neglecting studying the Bible (2 Timothy 2:15)

____ from a failure to glorify God (Ephesians 3:21)

____ from not having the attitude (mind) of Christ (Philippians 2:4–9)

____ from not caring for others (James 1:27; Galatians 6:10)

____ from failing to share the gospel (Mark 16:15–16)

____ from having a hardened heart (1 Timothy 4:1–7)

____ from associating with the evilness of the world (1 John 5:19)

____ from neglecting the assembly (Hebrews 10:24–25)

____ from not being on guard (1 Peter 5:8; Luke 8:12)

____ from not practicing love (1 Corinthians 13; 1 John)

____ from being afraid or being a coward (Acts 4:11–13)

____ from failing to bear fruit (Galatians 5:22–25)

Yes, it is clear from this short list that there are some Christians who need a wake-up call. How about you? What is your score?

What are some other areas in which Christians need a wake-up call? Let's all wake up and go forward pursuing the goals God has given us as His children. Remember, it has never been this late before as we move toward the midnight hour of judgment (Acts 17:30–31).

1

It Is Time to Wake Up

In her frustration, she entered the room with a third effort to get her husband to wake up and get out of bed.

"Harold, wake up! You are already late for work." Harold groaned and pulled the covers up over his head.

She continued, "They are waiting on you; they are depending on you to show up."

Harold pulled the covers from off his head and replied, "No! They don't like me. Nobody cares. It is just a waste of time."

"Harold, you've got to get up! You are the boss."

Many of us have had mornings like Harold had when we didn't want to wake up. Success in life depends on waking up, getting out of bed, and tackling the challenges of life.

We've all heard clichés like:

"Wake up and smell the coffee."
"Wake up and smell the roses."
"The early bird gets the worm."

Physical sleep is essential for good health, so nothing is wrong with getting an appropriate amount of sleep. When it is time to wake up, however, and we don't or haven't, our laziness can be disastrous.

It was the sixth of March 1987. The *Herald of Free Enterprise*, a ferry, was transporting cars between Dover, England, and Zeebrugge, Belgium. Cars were loaded through a front opening in the ship so they could be loaded onto the lower deck.

On that March winter night, with 563 passengers aboard, along with vehicles, Captain David Lewry put to sea. It was dark, 7:00 P.M. All went well in the safe harbor. But one mile out, ninety seconds after reaching the high seas, the ship capsized and sank within five minutes.

On that fatal night the ship had sailed with its front loading doors wide open. There was no indicator light on the bridge to alert the captain, so he had assumed the sailor responsible for closing the doors had done so. Instead, he was asleep in his cabin. Because assistant boatswain Mark Stanley was asleep on the job, 193 people died.

While sleep is essential, there are serious consequences from sleeping too much or at the wrong time. The wise man wrote these words to warn us:

> *He who gathers in summer is a wise son;*
> *He who sleeps in harvest*
> *is a son who causes shame.*
> —Proverbs 10:5

> *Do not love sleep, lest you come to poverty;*
> *Open your eyes, and you*
> *will be satisfied with bread.*
> —Proverbs 20:13

> *How long will you slumber, O sluggard?*
> *When will you rise from your sleep?*
> *A little sleep, a little slumber,*
> *A little folding of the hands to sleep—*
> *So shall your poverty come on you like a prowler,*
> *And your need like an armed man.*
> —Proverbs 6:9–11

> *Laziness casts one into a deep sleep,*
> *And an idle person will suffer hunger.*
> —Proverbs 19:15

While these truths are dynamic in a physical sense, they are far more so in a spiritual sense. Too much sleep may be dangerous in a physical sense, but it can have eternal consequences in a spiritual sense. That is why the apostle Paul warned,

"Awake, you who sleep, arise from the dead, and Christ will give you light" (Ephesians 5:14).

As Christians we are told to wake up. If we are asleep spiritually, we will suffer the consequences. The Bible is God's spiritual alarm clock for us. He has set it without a snooze button. We are called to be watchmen, to warn ourselves and others about the coming judgment of the Lord (Hebrews 9:27). But if we are lazy, sleeping watchmen, we are of little value. Here is how Isaiah described such watchmen:

> His watchmen are blind, they are all ignorant; they are all dumb dogs, they cannot bark; sleeping, lying down, loving to slumber (Isaiah 56:10).

A reading of Ezekiel 3:17–21 will educate us to the duties of a watchman.

When Jesus was in the garden praying to His Father about His death on the cross, He asked Peter, James, and John to watch with Him (Mark 14:34).

> Then He came and found them sleeping, and said to Peter, "Simon, are you sleeping? Could you not watch an hour? Watch and pray . . . " (Mark 14:37–41).

When Jesus needs us the most, are we asleep? Are we sleeping when we should be praying? Have we turned off the spiritual alarm clock? Do we keep pushing the snooze button? Are we waiting for a tomorrow when we will arise and be about our Master's business?

The ad said for $9.99 per month you would receive one daily wake-up call and three snooze calls. Other ads offered more expensive and cheaper wake-up calls. Our wake-up call as Christians is the most expensive of all: the blood of Christ (Matthew 26:28). There is no snooze button because, if we love Him we will keep His commandments (John 14:15).

Jesus came to Israel to give them a wake-up call. But they didn't accept it. In Matthew 16:1–6 He rebuked the Pharisees and Sadducees by reminding them that they knew how to read the signs of the weather, but they didn't know how to tell what time it was for them. Spiritually and receptively speaking, it was the time of the Messiah. It was the fullness of time (Galatians 4:4). They failed to heed His wake-up calls and suf-

fered the consequences in the destruction of Jerusalem in
A.D. 70.

Christians, wake up!

Open your eyes to the condition of the world and churches.
It has been said that only 17 percent of Americans attend
church on any given Sunday. Atheism is the fastest growing
religion in America. More church doors are closing than new
ones are opening in America. Launched by the Master's march-
ing orders to go into the whole world and preach the gospel
(Mark 16:15–16), we have taken sanctuary in our buildings
and complained about how dark it is outside. We have been
arguing about deck chairs while the old ship of Zion is sinking. We have failed to realize that it has never been this late
before.

Christians, wake up!

The battle is raging; crew members are abandoning the
battleship or booking passage on cruise ships where the food
buffet is open so passengers can pick and choose the theological diets they prefer. A paid crew takes care of all the duties,
while we enjoy the fun and games created and led by cruise
counselors. No one is manning the battle stations.

Christians, wake up!

Today!

Yesterday is gone and
only lives as a memory:
good or bad.

Tomorrow is not here yet;
it is only a vague promise
that may or may not
come true.

Today! Today is here,
it is ours to use
and enjoy in the
now moments of life.

So today I will wake up,
stay awake and pursue
God's best for my life.

I say with the psalmist:
'This is the day the Lord has made,
I will rejoice and be glad in it.'

Today I am awake and fully alive!

—J. J. Turner

We all need wake-up calls. Stephen Covey wrote, "In the absence of wake-up calls, many of us never really confront the critical issues of life." Life is lived in the present, in the here and now; we must free ourselves of all the foolish and useless trivia and make room for living and loving as God has commanded. We must develop the habit of living each day as if it is our last. Why? Because one of these days our names will be called and we will exit from death row into eternity. This should be a major reason to wake up. We need to get on with living for the Lord; we don't have forever.

Christians, wake up!

We may know many things, from the *Theory of Relativity* to the formulas of DNA. We may create new and exciting inventions and master languages and other skills, yet not know who we are at the soul level. The need of the hour is for us Christians to dig deeply into our souls and acknowledge that we need a fresh wake-up call from God. We need to say with the psalmist, "Lord, will You not revive me again?" And He answers, "Yes, but only if you want to be revived."

Why It Is Time to Wake Up

There are numerous reasons for us to consider seriously the need to wake up. Here are a few:

1. Because God has commanded it in His word.

2. Because of the many needs in a lost world.

3. Because of the consequences of not waking up.

4. Because many congregations are asleep and need to wake up.

5. Because of the challenges of our changing times.

6. Because our enemy, Satan, never sleeps (1 Peter 5:8).

7. Because the church in many quarters is being led into apostasy.

8. Because the number of workers is getting smaller.

9. Because we have a covenant agreement to be faithful unto death (Revelation 2:10).

10. Because it has never been this late before.

11. Because we have an eternal responsibility.

12. Because we want to be like our Father: He never sleeps.

For Thought and Discussion

1. How do you handle physical wake-up calls?

2. What is the most annoying wake-up call you've received?

3. What is a spiritual wake-up call?

4. In what sense does the church need a wake-up call?

5. What will you do if you discover you need a wake-up call?

6. How has Satan lulled us to sleep?

7. What is spiritual snoozing?

8. What are some additional reasons for waking up spiritually?

9. Why do some Christians refuse to wake up?

10. What additional observations do you have?

Lord, Wake Me Up!

Lord, if I slumber,
Wake me up.
Lord, if I snooze,
Wake me up.
Lord, if I am neglecting
My responsibilities,
Wake me up.
Lord, if there is a need
I don't see, wake me up.
Lord, if I have blind spots,
Wake me up.
Lord, if I have been neglecting
My prayer life,
Wake me up.
Lord, if my zeal is cooling,
Wake me up.
Lord, if my faith is in a comfort zone,
Wake me up.
Lord, if I stray from Your word,
Wake me up.
Lord, if I fail to do good unto all men,
Wake me up.
Lord, if I have failed to see the hurts
Around me, wake me up.
Lord, if I wane in my love for You
And for my neighbor, wake me up.
Lord, if I fail to put Your
Kingdom first, wake me up.
Lord, just keep me awake all the time,
Be my constant alarm—*please*.
—J. J. Turner

2

It Has Never Been This Late

What Time Is It?

Have you ever noticed how frequently we ask and answer this question related to time?

I'll date myself. When I was a boy my favorite after-school TV program was always introduced by a character named Buffalo Bob. He would ask in a loud voice, "Boys and girls, what time is it!" The kids in the peanut gallery would shout back, "It's Howdy Doody time!"

Time! It's the stuff life is made of. Time is a continual state of flow—moving forward. We erroneously use the phrase "manage time" as though we can collect it and hold it until needed in the future. Not so. We use the present moment of time either wisely or foolishly; we manage our behavior relative to the usage of time.

What Time Is It?

What time is it?
Time to do well,
Time to live better,
Give up that grudge,
Answer that letter,
Speak the kind word to
Sweeten a sorrow,
Do that good deed you
Would leave till tomorrow.
—Author unknown

Since this study is about wake-up calls, we need to ask: What is a wake-up call? In its noun form, a wake-up call is defined as "a warning to take action, concerning something that has been overlooked or neglected." It is also defined as "a telephone call that you request at a specific time in order to wake up at that time; especially in hotels." For example, "Sir, do you need a wake-up call in the morning?"

What time is it? In the scheme of life, it has never been this late before, and each minute makes it later and later in our journey to eternity.

Ethel and Herman was a typical farming couple. They worked from sunup to sundown, five days a week on their farm. Come Saturday, as most couples like to do if possible, they tried to sleep in. One Saturday morning they were lying in bed trying to sleep, which was difficult after getting up every morning at five. Ethel was in a snoring mode, but Herman was tossing and turning. As he was tossing and turning, the old grandfather clock in the living room started donging. And it kept on striking. Something was wrong! Herman started to count the dongs. Dong 10, dong 11, dong 12! When the clock donged the seventeenth time, Herman reached over and shook Ethel and shouted, "Get up Ethel! Wake up! It's later than it has ever been!"

In a chronometry sense, Herman was wrong, but in a spiritual and realistic sense, he was right: *It has never been this late.* We have never had this day, hour, minute, or second before. That is why it is critical for Christians to wake up to the challenges the church and gospel are facing every day.

A National Wake-Up Call

Do you remember where you were on the morning of September 11, 2001? That day the United States received a major wake-up call. I remember where I was. I had stopped at McDonald's in Denver to grab a cup of coffee. I was inside at the counter when a man in line behind me asked if I heard about the plane crash in New York City. I hadn't. Over in a corner, a TV flashed a news bulletin informing the nation that two planes had crashed into the Twin Towers in New York City. Later we learned that the unthinkable had happened.

Terrorists had done what we assumed was impossible—attacked us on our own soil. Our nation has never been the same since that fatal day.

Almost two years into the twenty-first century, the United States of America experienced vulnerability and pain never before known by this generation. The whole nation reacted in tears, sorrow, outrage, and countless falling on its knees in prayer, led by the President. Church attendance soared. America was returning to her roots—asking God for help and guidance. Acts of heroism were common as people, without thinking about their own safety, rushed to help others.

A number of things resulted from the wake-up call of 9/11:

- We became a united nation.
- We became a praying nation.
- We again recognized that human life was prized highly.
- We found security in our families as they were drawn closer together.
- We found security in the new Homeland Security.
- We noticed new security and permanent changes in air travel.
- We developed a greater mistrust of our foreign neighbors.
- We acknowledged we had an ongoing enemy: Terrorism.
- We plunged into war with Iraq.
- We welcomed new security measures on a global level.

Sadly, many of the positive effects of the 9/11 wake-up call, such as prayer and unity of the nation, quickly fell by the wayside. Our nation soon divided over the war and many issues of national defense and security, and political parties began ripping one another to shreds. We soon drifted back to sleep or snoozing relative to the real needs of our nation. Jesus Christ reminded us two thousand years ago that that a house divided against itself can't stand (Matthew 12:25).

Like most Americans, I paused to write my response to the tragic events of 9/11. Here is my poetic response:

I Saw America Cry

Who can ever forget that fatal day
Now called 9/11? When we were
Attacked, molested, raped, and killed;
Innocent blood shed for no reason.

The news commentator tried to report
The mayhem perpetrated by cowards
From a distant shore, with tears slowly
Running down his cheeks:
I saw America cry.

In the cornfields of Iowa,
And on Gulf Shore boats:
I saw America cry.

On the crowded LA freeways
And on the open Texas highways:
I saw America cry.

From the shores of Maine
To the shores of Washington State:
I saw America cry.

From the classrooms in Georgia
To the dorms in Ohio:
I saw America cry.

From the brave cop on the beat
To the little old lady in church:
I saw America cry.

The President led us in prayer
As our politicians bowed their knees:
I saw America cry.

America cried because she was
Hurt, angry, and lost for a moment.
She cried because her sons and daughters
Had been taken to early graves
And robbed of a future.

America cried because fathers
And mothers weren't coming home again;

Plans for a future together were
Sent to silent graves never to return.

As I looked at myself in the mirror
Reflecting on the tragedy of 9/11:
I cried with America.

—2001 J. J. Turner

Our nation needs a wake-up call. Evidently a lot of people agree with this observation, as there are in excess of 39 million hits on websites when you type in the search engine the words "Wake up, America." A lot of people and groups are trying to sound the alarm. I pray that America will not require that alarm to come in the middle of the night in the form of a terrorist act but that it will come from the lips of righteous people—God's people—Christians.

The following poem was reportedly written by an Arizona student, but no matter who wrote it, it has a powerful message that hits home:

Now I sit me down in school
Where praying is against the rule,
For this great nation under God
Finds mention of Him very odd.

If Scripture now the class recites,
It violates the Bill of Rights.
And anytime my head I bow
Becomes a federal matter now.

Our hair can be purple, orange, or green,
There's no offense; it's a freedom scene.
The law is specific; the law is precise.
Prayers spoken aloud are a serious vice.

For praying in a public hall
Might offend someone with no faith at all.
In silence alone we must meditate,
God's name is prohibited by the state.

We're allowed to curse and dress like freaks,
And pierce our noses, tongues, and cheeks.

They've outlawed guns, but first the Bible,
To quote the Good Book makes me liable.

We can elect a pregnant Senior Queen,
And the "unwed daddy," our Senior King.
It's "inappropriate" to teach right from wrong;
We're taught that "judgments" do not belong.

We can get our condoms and birth controls,
Study witchcraft, vampires, and totem poles,
But the Ten Commandments are not allowed;
No word of God must reach this crowd.

It's scary here I must confess,
When chaos reigns, the school's a mess;
So, Lord, this silent plea I make:
Should I be shot: My soul please take! Amen.

As Christians, may we wake up and stand firm for our great constitutional heritage and those biblical and moral principles that our founders laid as a foundation for our survival as a beacon light to the world. It is later than it has ever been.

What You Miss While You Sleep

Have you ever slept through an important event or opportunity? Or have you missed something important because you didn't wake up in time? Most of us have. Remember the saying, "If you snooze you lose"?

There is no telling what you may miss because of a failure to wake up. Years ago the Associated Press released a story about Gene Tipps, a twenty-year-old man of Seymour, Texas. He received several serious head injuries in a car wreck. After three weeks in a coma, he remained the next eight years in a state of unconsciousness. During that time he received careful attention from his family and medical people.

Then one day after all these years of "sleep," he woke up. Obviously everyone was startled but thankful. Imagine what it must have been like for him.

Later when he was asked questions about being asleep for eight years, Mr. Tipps replied, "It is all very strange. My girlfriend is now married with children, and the war in Vietnam is over. To everyone else I am twenty-eight, but in my mind I am still twenty." As he slept from 1967 to 1975, he stepped from Lyndon Johnson's presidency to Jimmy Carter's. He slept right through the Nixon presidential years.

Physically, it's amazing what you miss while asleep, either for a short period or a long one. Life moves on with all its ups and downs. But do you know what is more amazing? What is missed while we sleep spiritually? Those things are eternally important, so we need to sound the alarm for Christians to wake up. It has never been this late spiritually.

The Church Needs a Wake-Up Call

Do you know where the first example of someone physically sleeping during worship is located in your Bible? It is in Acts 20:8–9.

> There were many lamps in the upper room where they were gathered together. And in a window sat a certain young man named Eutychus, who was sinking into deep sleep. He was overcome by sleep; and as Paul continued speaking, he fell down from the third story and was taken up dead.

How blessed this young man was that Paul was there to raise him from the dead!

Christians need to wake up. Why? Again, it has never been this late. This old ball of dirt is spinning with a population destined to reach seven billion souls in 2012, most of whom are lost and unprepared to take the trip to the silent city. The church is falling further and further behind in taking the gospel to every person in the world as Jesus commanded (Mark 16:15–16). The words of our late brother Clayton Pepper still echo in my ears: "Evangelism is the last thing we practice and the first thing we abandon."

The decline of involvement in church is apalling. On any given Sunday it is estimated that only about seventeen percent of Americans attend church. The divorce rate among Christians is higher than the rate among atheists. An evening watching of the global news dumps an amazing assortment of illustrations showing the results of every sin imaginable.

The church can wake up only to the degree that each member wakes up. A comparison of the teachings of the Bible and the practices of those claiming to follow it is alarming. Biblical Christianity has been exchanged for "churchanity": going through a set of rituals that has very little impact on life and character out in the real world.

The Bible affirms that the local church is the focal point for displaying God's glory, love, and redemption to the world (Ephesians 3:21). If God's called-out people—the church—don't do it, it won't get done. Each member in every local congregation should reflect a commitment to living and sharing the gospel (cf. Romans 1:14–16).

As Christians, we must wake up to the reality of the state of the world and the local church. We must not snooze through the battle cry to arise and put our armor on. We are closer to the midnight hour of eternal judgment than we have ever been. Weak, compromising Christians will not win the battle against wickedness in high places.

Christians, wake up! It has never been this late.

For Thought and Discussion

1. What comes to your mind when you hear the words "wake-up call"?

2. What is your evaluation of what time it is in America today?

3. Why do we tend to "sleep" in face of challenges?

4. How did 9/11 affect our nation?

5. How long did we stay awake after 9/11?

6. What spiritual message is there in 9/11 for us? Why?

7. Why do Christians need a wake-up call?

8. How can we awaken the church to her duties?

9. What additional observations do you have?

10. What one intentional thing do you plan to do because of this lesson?

CHAPTER

3

Is This All There Is
to Christianity?

Have you ever caught yourself sitting in church services wondering if attendance, singing, giving, and partaking of the Lord's supper are all God is expecting of you as a Christian? I confess it has happened to me numerous times on my journey with Christ. I also admit that as I have taught and preached for forty-five years, as I have looked over my audiences, I have wondered, Is this all there is? Was this the end God had in mind when He sent His Son to die on a cross? Is being in the audience on Sunday world-changing? I think not!

Why are many Christians dropping out of church? Why does a percentage of them, when asked why, respond by saying they are bored or not challenged. One member said, "Attending church is like watching the same old movie over and over every week. You know the plot inside and out. Surely there is more to Christianity than running in circles week after week."

Somewhere between the air-conditioned foyer and padded pews, Christianity lost its mantra: They who "live godly in Christ Jesus shall suffer persecution." While trying to win friends and influence people, we have failed to make enemies because we tell people the truth (Galatians 4:16). We stand by and watch our neighbor's house burn and never cry, Fire! We fear fire and therefore fail to snatch men "out of the fire" (Jude 23).

We have all heard the jokes about members sleeping in church. While it is a physical possibility that many engage in, there is also the possibility of sleeping spiritually in the assembly. Paul wrote these words to the Christians in Ephesus: "Awake, you who sleep, arise from the dead, and Christ will give you light" (Ephesians 5:14). Because of their abuse of the Lord's supper, Paul issued this warning to the Christians in Corinth: "For this reason many are weak and sick among you, *and many sleep"* (1 Corinthians 11:30).

Proof that many in the church need a wake-up call is evidenced by the fact that in many congregations 10 to 20 percent of the members do all the work, while the other 80 to 90 percent enjoy and benefit from their labors. Is that what God intended? Every member has a responsibility to contribute to the mission of the local church. To the Ephesians who were challenged by unity issues, Paul wrote this description of the responsibility of every member to do something:

> . . . from whom the whole body, joined and knit together by what every joint supplies, according to the effective working by which every member does its share, causes growth of the body for the edifying of itself in love (Ephesians 4:16).

According to this verse, there is no such thing as an inactive, irresponsible member in the body of Christ. Every member must supply something. "To whom much has been committed, of him they will ask the more" (Luke 12:48).

Using the analogy of the physical body, we know that when a member of the body stops functioning, it is considered sick or diseased and in need of medical attention.

What Christianity Is Not About

If a person does not know what Christianity is about, how can he or she go about practicing it as God desires? While it is true that we will spend our spiritual lives learning more and more about what Christianity involves, there are some things we can know rather quickly. These things are learned by discovering some of the things Christianity is not about. We must wake up to these things.

1. Christianity is not about auditing God's word—it is about being a doer of God's word (James 2:21–23).

2. Christianity is not about arbitrarily judging the actions of others—it is about preparing for the judgment at which we will all appear, giving an account of the deeds done in our bodies (Matthew 7:1–7; Hebrews 9:27; Acts 17:30–31).

3. Christianity is not about who can give the most—it is about giving our bodies as a living sacrifice to God (Romans 12:1–2).

4. Christianity is not about being like those in the world around us—it is about being transformed (Romans 12:2).

5. Christianity is not about being a workaholic or trying to earn one's salvation—it is about leading a balanced life and accepting God's amazing grace (Ephesians 2:5–9; Mark 6: 30–32).

6. Christianity is not about hording the seed of the kingdom in a church building—it is about sowing the seed in the entire world (Luke 8:10–15; Mark 16:15–16).

7. Christianity is not about only attending functions at the church building several hours a week—it is about serving God 24-7-365 (Galatians 6:10; James 1:27; Revelation 2:10).

Obviously this list could go on and on, but these seven observations should awaken us to the fact that Christianity is more involved and demanding than some have thought. The spiritual alarm clock is sounding and it's time to wake up and get more involved in kingdom business (Luke 2:48–52). Are you fully awake?

What Is Christianity About?

Is it possible for one to become a Christian and not have any idea what Christianity is all about? From a human perspective, I guess so, but from a Bible perspective the answer is no.

Every person who becomes a Christian, with perhaps a rare exception, does so with a preconceived idea or concept of what Christianity is all about. Many spend the rest of their spiritual lives trying to live in harmony with their concepts; occasionally, they will change or adjust their concept or understanding.

Once while knocking doors in a campaign, I came to a yard where several bikers were enjoying life. When one of them discovered I was from a local church, he said, "Man, Christ was an all-right dude and Christianity is cool." Inside I flinched, but outwardly I maintained my composure, thinking, Christianity is anything but cool. It is about a cross. How can a cruel death on a cross be cool? Jesus placed the cross as the litmus test for His followers: "If anyone desires to follow after Me, let him deny himself, and take up his cross, and follow Me" (Matthew 16:24).

For many today the cross is only a piece of jewelry. For others it is a point of argument as to whether or not it should be placed as an ornament on a church building. I once heard a missionary tell a story about the ending of an Easter celebration in Brazil. As the day was drawing to a close and people were leaving the square where a giant cathedral had received thousands of visitors, the merchandise hawkers were lowering their prices in order to get rid of the goods they had brought to sell to the pilgrims. The missionary said one voice was audible above all the crying salesmen. One man was screaming, "Hey, cheap crosses for sell! Get your cheap crosses! They will never be cheaper! Cheap crosses for sale!"

The cross is not cheap. It must not be interpreted as an easy way to follow Jesus for fishes and loaves. Today it is the equivalent of saying, "If any man will come after me, let him sit in the electric chair, or be hanged on a gallows." Christianity is about the daily carrying of a cross because of a denial of self. This is no easy task.

Cruise Ship or Battleship?

Some think of Christianity as a pleasure journey on a cruise ship—a place for fun and games. You may rest, play, and relax at your own leisure. You may go through a buffet line and choose foods that suit your taste. It seems like every day there is a mass exit from the battleship where the demands are tough, to a berth on the cruise ship. Paul targeted this spirit with these words:

> Preach the word . . . For the time will come when they will not endure sound doctrine, but according to their own desires, because they have itching ears, they will heap up for themselves teachers; and they will turn their ears away from the truth, and be turned to fables (2 Timothy 4:2–4).

Following Christ—that is what the name Christianity implies—is not about having it easy. It is about suffering, cross-bearing, and fighting the fight of faith. "All who desire to live godly in Christ Jesus will suffer persecution" (2 Timothy 3:12). Peter wrote, "Yet if anyone suffers as a Christian, let him not be ashamed, but let him glorify God in this matter" (1 Peter 4:16).

We need to wake up and realize that Christianity is about a spiritual warfare. Paul wrote,

> For we do not wrestle against flesh and blood, but against principalities, against powers, against the rulers of the darkness of this age, against spiritual hosts of wickedness in the heavenly places (Ephesians 6:12).

Satan is the general leading the forces of darkness that we are battling. "Be sober, be vigilant; because your adversary the devil walks about like a roaring lion, seeking whom he may devour" (1 Peter 5:8).

Christianity is about a lifelong journey in faith. The Hebrews writer makes this clear with these words:

> But without faith it is impossible to please Him, for he who comes to God must believe that He is, and that He is a rewarder of those who diligently seek Him (Hebrews 11:6).

You may have a lot of things going for you, such as money, position, looks, authority, knowledge, speaking ability, and knowledge of the biblical languages, Greek and Hebrew, but without faith your batting average is zero: "Without faith it is impossible to please God." This is why we must "walk by faith, not by sight." The walk of faith must continue through death (Revelation 2:10).

God Is Not a Cosmic Bookkeeper

Another thing Christianity is all about is knowing God. In fact, this is the beginning point. Jesus, in prayer to His Father, said, "And this is eternal life, that they may know You, the only true God, and Jesus Christ whom You have sent" (John 17:3).

One may know 101 facts about God and still not know Him in an intimate and personal way. To some He is no more than a cosmic bookkeeper who resides outside this world; He has a little black book in which He delights in keeping records of our wrongs so He can punish us. Paul had the opposite attitude when he wrote,

> For this reason I also suffer these things; nevertheless I am not ashamed, for I know whom I have believed and am persuaded that He is able to keep what I have committed to Him until that Day (2 Timothy 1:12).

The lifelong goal of Bible study is to learn more and more about God so you can function as a doer of the word (James 1:21–24).

Christianity is about knowing and doing God's will. It is in harmony with the attitude of Christ in the garden when He prayed, "Nevertheless, not My will, but Yours, be done." God's will for His children is contained in His word, the Bible. As our Father, He is concerned about every action of His children. James called this to our attention with these words to those who were leaving God's will out of their plans:

> Come now, you who say, "Today or tomorrow we will go to such and such a city, spend a year there, buy and sell, and make a profit"; whereas you do not know what will happen tomorrow. For what is your life? It is even a vapor that appears for a little time and then vanishes away. Instead you ought to say, "If the Lord wills, we shall live and do this or that" (James 4:13–15).

"I have slept through most of my Christian life," Larry said as he sat weeping on the front pew, having come before the congregation asking for prayer as he rededicated his life to God's service. I wonder how many others are asleep relative to God's will for their lives.

Signs You May Be Asleep

When a person is asleep physically there are several signs. He may be snoring, he may be nodding his head, he may be unresponsive to words, or he may be lying in bed. Some of Webster's definitions of nonphysical sleep are "to be dormant, quiescent, or inactive, as faculties; to be careless or not alert; to allow one's alertness, vigilance, or attentiveness to lie dormant." That sounds like what the apostle Peter was warning against in his epistle (1 Peter 5:8). We must be sober and awake, manning our battle stations for the good fight of faith.

How can you know if you are spiritually asleep? Here are few possible signs:

1. You may be letting God's call to action go unheeded. Oh yes, you plan to get more involved—tomorrow.

2. You are still bound by pre-Christian habits; there has been no growth and little change in your life.

3. You may be starving and not know you need a better diet of God's nourishing word (Matthew 4:4).

4. You may have forgotten what it means to seek the kingdom first, if you ever knew (Matthew 6:33). It means to put God and His business first in your life (Luke 2:50–52).

5. You may have grown cold in the Lord's work. Check your temperature. Are you ( ) hot, ( ) lukewarm, or ( ) cold? Read Revelation 3:14–22. God wants us to be "zealous" (hot) relative to His assigned works.

6. You might no longer be touched by the gospel. Oh yes, you go to church services and listen to the preacher, but for some reason you are not moved by God's preached word. Could it be that you have reached "a point of no return," that your "conscience is seared with a hot iron"? (1 Timothy 4:2).

7. You might no longer by moved by the cross, if you ever were. It is just another familiar Bible story (John 12:32; Romans 1:14–16).

Remember the story of Rip Van Winkle by Washington Irving? Rip was a ne'er-do-well who slept for twenty years and upon waking was startled to discover how much the world had changed. If the world in the early 1800s had changed drastically, imagine what Rip would discover today if he were to awake from a twenty-year nap.

In a metaphorical sense, many in the church today are suffering from the Rip Van Winkle syndrome. They are asleep, spiritually speaking. They are just the opposite of the men of Issachar "who had understanding of the times, to know what Israel ought to do" (1 Chronicles 12:32).

As world population rocks close to the seven billion mark, the body of Christ is shrinking. Once-large churches are loosing members. Some are thinking about closing their doors, and others are worried about how to stem the loss in membership. What's wrong? What's happening? Whatever the answers might be, it is obviously going to take an awake Christianity to provide the solution. This is only possible as one by one, Christians wake up and respond to the battle cry to go forward sowing seed in the hearts of the lost (cf. Luke 8:11–19). Seed must not be kept safely in barns (church buildings). They must be scattered throughout the world. We plant and water, and God gives the increase. That is His method of demonstrating that we are awake and active (1 Corinthians 3:4–9).

For Thought and Discussion

1. Why is the mission of the church misunderstood by some members?

2. How does a preconceived idea about Christianity influence one's Christian life?

3. Where did the idea originate that church attendance is all that matters?

4. In your own words write a statement of what you believe Christianity is about.

_____

_____

_____

5. Discuss the Rip Van Winkle syndrome and how it applies to today.

6. How would you describe your present state relative to being awake: ( ) hot ( ) lukewarm ( ) cold ( ) not sure?

7. How can we wake up those who are asleep?

8. What additional observations do you have?

9. How do you plan to use this lesson in your life?

CHAPTER

4

Is Christianity
Riding the Titanic?

Whether it is true or not, the common belief is that Nero fiddled while Rome burned. The band played on while the *Titanic* sank. History now notes that we could have possibly prevented the Japanese attack on Pearl Harbor in 1941. Jesus warned and challenged five of the seven churches in Asia Minor to repent. None of the seven exist today, not even those who had no negative marks. Sadly, the same is true of the many other churches we read about in the New Testament:

1. Where is the church in Philippi?
2. Where is the church in Corinth?
3. Where is the church in Antioch?
4. Where is the church in Thessalonica?
5. Where is the church in Colosse?
6. Where is the church in Rome?
7. Where is the church in Galatia?

How about our day? How is the church? Is the bride of Christ growing? Statistics say no. Is the body of Christ having a major influence on our sinful world for righteousness? A lack of fruit says no. What's wrong? We have more resources than ever; yet we seem to be falling further and further behind. Is Christianity as we know it today riding the *Titanic*? Are we sinking in a sea of apathy? There is widespread belief that Christianity of an evangelical nature is doomed. Like it or not, accept it or not, we are placed in the category with other conservative groups under the Christian umbrella called evangelical.

In the March 10, 2009, edition of *Christian Science Monitor*, Michael Spencer of Oneida, Kentucky, wrote:

> We are on the verge—within 10 years—of a major collapse of evangelical Christianity. This breakdown will follow the deterioration of the mainline Protestant world and it will fundamentally alter the religious and cultural environment in the West.
>
> Within two generations, evangelicalism will be a house deserted of half its occupants. (Between 25 and 35 percent of Americans today are Evangelicals). In the "Protestant" 20th century, Evangelicals flourished. But they will soon be living in a very secular and religiously antagonistic 21st century.
>
> This collapse will herald the arrival of an anti-Christian chapter of the post-Christian West. Intolerance of Christianity will rise to levels many of us have not believed possible in our lifetimes, and public policy will become hostile toward evangelical Christianity, seeing it as the opponent of the common good.
>
> Millions of Evangelicals will quit. Thousands of ministries will end. Christian media will be reduced, if not eliminated. Many Christian schools will go into rapid decline. I'm convinced the grace and mission of God will reach to the ends of the earth. But the end of evangelicalism as we know it is close.

In the article, Spencer gives seven answers to the question: Why is this going to happen?

1. Evangelicals have identified their movement with the culture war and with political conservatism.

2. We Evangelicals have failed to pass on to our young people an orthodox form of faith that can take root and survive the secular onslaught.

3. There are three kinds of evangelical churches today: consumer-driven mega churches, dying churches, and new churches whose future is fragile.

4. Despite some very successful developments in the past 25 years, Christian education has not produced a product that can withstand the rising tide of secularism.

5. The confrontation between cultural secularism and the faith at the core of evangelical efforts to "do good" is rapidly approaching.

6. Even in areas where Evangelicals imagine themselves strong—in the Bible Belt, for example—we will find a great inability to pass on to our children a vital evangelical confidence in the Bible and the importance of the faith.

7. The money will dry up.

While we may choose not to be identified with so-called evangelicals, we have a similar set of challenges. Wake up! Take a look around and you will see that these seven reasons are on our doorsteps if not already in our house. Ignoring the creeping darkness will not bring light.

Christianity is riding the *Titanic* only if we choose to ignore the warning signs and fail to respond in a biblical manner. The church *must* wake up, and she can only do so as her members, one by one, wake up. If our leaders are asleep in the captain's comfortable quarters, our deckhands are watching the game, and the dieticians are preparing snacks and fast foods, we are taking on water and sinking is up ahead.

Plug the Holes

> Soldiers of Christ, arise
> And put your armor on;
> Strong in the strength which God supplies,
> Strong in the strength which God's supplies
> Thro' His beloved Son.
> —Charles Wesley

It is time to man our battle stations. Why? In the words of Paul, "The night is far spent, the day is at hand. Therefore let us cast off the works of darkness, and let us put on the armor of light. Let us walk properly in the day" (Romans 13:12–13).

We must not faint or grow discouraged, so we are faced with many challenges. That has always been the case. Reread Acts. Jesus promised that the "gates of hell" would not prevail against the church (Matthew 16:16–24). While we know that is true of the universal body of Christ, many local congregations are in danger of sinking. They must plug the holes that are letting the ship take on water.

1. We need to plug the hole that is robbing us of a commitment to Bible study (2 Timothy 2:15).

2. We need to plug the hole that is contributing to a lack of attendance in all services (Hebrews 10:24–25).

3. We need to plug the hole that is preventing the kingdom from being first in our lives (Matthew 6:33).

4. We need to plug the hole that is contributing to our indifference to the needs of others, both in and out of the church (James 1:27; Galatians 6:10).

5. We need to plug the hole of reluctance to share the gospel with the lost (Mark 16:15–16; Luke 19:10).

6. We need to plug the hole that is preventing us from having the attitude of Christ in every situation (Philippians 2:4–9).

7. We need to plug the holes of unfaithfulness and become doers of the word (Revelation 2:10; James 1:22–24).

8. We need to plug the hole that is keeping us from being the prayer warriors we need to be (1 Thessalonians 5:17).

9. We need to plug the hole that is contributing to our status quo approach to the mission of the church (Matthew 28:18–20).

10. We need to plug the hole that is prohibiting us from seriously taking worship as a way of life and devotion to God. One to three hours per week isn't enough (Romans 12:1; John 4:23–24).

The waters of indifference and noninvolvement can seep slowly into the Old Ship of Zion, and before we know it, she will sink. The challenge is for us to awaken to this truth and to be on guard against potential holes in her spiritual hull.

Dressed for Battle

When the call comes over the ship's PA system, "Man your battle stations!" it is serious. Imagine some sailors deciding to "sleep in," some taking their time getting dressed, others playing cards, and still others rushing to get ready for battle. That scene would be disastrous and lead to chaos, loss of life, and perhaps the sinking of the ship. Court martials would follow promptly.

During war time soldiers and sailors sleep in their battle gear; they are ready at an instant's notice to engage the enemy. Since each Christian is a soldier in the Lord's army, it is imperative that readiness be a characteristic of our daily lives. We must always be dressed for spiritual battle.

Here is Paul's admonition to the Lord's army in Ephesus:

> Put on the whole armor of God, that you may be able to stand against the wiles of the devil. For we do not wrestle against flesh and blood, but against principalities, against powers, against the rulers of the darkness of this age, against spiritual hosts of wickedness in the heavenly places. Therefore take up the whole armor of God, that you may be able to withstand in the evil day, and having done all, to stand (Ephesians 6:11–13).

If we think things were rough and evil in Paul's day, a casual look around will reveal that we are living in a sinful world with more ways of sinning than ever before. The world is shifting under our feet; it is difficult to find a safe place to stand. Thankfully, we have the sure foundation of Christ upon which to stand (1 Corinthians 3:1–13). In the midst of this revolutionary shift in values, morals, and respect for authority of any kind, Christians find themselves stationed in a battle mode. It's high time that we wake up to the challenges facing us in a worried, unsettled, nervous, shaken, and hostile world. The church must not be hiding in caves trying to exist in the dinosaur mode of the past.

We must be dressed for battle 24-7-365. Casual clothes such as swim suits, walking shorts, sweats, and jeans won't help us defeat the enemy. After warning us about our enemy—Satan—

the apostle Paul reminds us how we must be dressed in order to participate effectively in warfare:

> Stand therefore, having girded your waist with truth, having put on the breastplate of righteousness, and having shod your feet with the preparation of the gospel of peace; above all, taking the shield of faith with which you will be able to quench all the fiery darts of the wicked one. And take the helmet of salvation, and the sword of the Spirit, which is the word of God; praying always with all prayer and supplication in the Spirit, being watchful to this end with all perseverance and supplication for all the saints (Ephesians 6:14–18).

While the modern world has a new set of devices to entice, capture, and destroy, the ancient armor of God is still sufficient to defeat the enemy. The challenge is to outfit oneself with the powerful weapons of God. This requires dedication, determination, and hard work, qualities that are lacking in many Christians.

It is time to wake up and man our battle stations.

Too Many Irons in the Fire

One of today's most popular excuses for not being engaged in the war against our enemy is, "I'm too busy." As soldiers of Christ, our priorities are clearly defined by our "battle manual":

> You therefore, my son, be strong in the grace that is in Christ Jesus. And the things that you have heard from me among many witnesses, commit these to faithful men who will be able to teach others also. You therefore must endure hardship as a good soldier (2 Timothy 2:1–3).

Jesus made it clear that our singular allegiance must be to the kingdom of God (Matthew 6:33). He also made it clear that there would be no place for excuses or cop-outs relative to following Him. Jesus taught several parables in which He made it clear that excuses would not be accepted (Luke 9:57–62; 14:12–24).

Excuse making has become so popular there is even a book that has numerous excuses you may use in order to get out of work, obligations, and responsibilities. Christians have their own list of excuses:

"My son had to play in a ball game."
"Relatives came into town at the last minute."
"I didn't hear about it until it was too late."
"I wasn't feeling well."
"I didn't have the right clothes."
"I had to work late."
"I have taken on an extra job."

Complex situations will arise that will hinder or prevent one from being engaged in some particular mission of the church, but they must not become perpetual excuses. We must wake up to the fact that having too many irons in the fire isn't spiritually healthy. It is okay to be busy if it is in the tenor of Jesus, who at age twelve said, "Why did you seek Me? Did you not know that I must be about my Father's business?" (Luke 2:49).

Have We Lost Our Identity?

Do we Christians know who we are? Does the church have a clear vision of who she is and what her mission is in the world? In his book, *Escape from Church, Inc.*, E. Glenn Wagner addresses this point:

> No matter how you look at the statistics, they seem to point to the same conclusion: The American church exerts precious little influence on society. Not only is church growth failing to keep up with the nation's birthrate, but the behavior of those who identify themselves as Christians cannot be distinguished statistically from those who make no such claims (Zondervan Publishing House, 1999, p. 18).

How can we be the "light of the world" or a "city set on a hill" if we don't know who and why we are? Psychology tells us that we act in harmony with our perceptions and self-image. If we don't see ourselves as a battleship in a life-and-death struggle for souls, how will we ever storm the fortresses of the devil? So long as we perceive ourselves as just one of many self-help groups in town trying to entice members, we will never be martyrs carrying a cross in the footsteps of our Master (1 Peter 2:21).

We must wake up to our identity as soldiers of Christ, and stop acting as cruise directors on the "Good Ship Lollipop." Christianity is not riding the *Titanic*. We are "in Christ" (Galatians 3:27) where power flows and victory is assured, that is, if we sail on faithfully unto death (Ephesians 3:20–21; Revelation 2:10).

For Thought and Discussion

1. With what has the word *Titanic* become synonymous?

2. Why did the churches mentioned in the New Testament cease to exist?

3. What would you say the overall basic health of the church is today?

4. What is your reaction to the word *Evangelical*? Why are we placed in the category?

5. What are your thoughts on Michael Spencer's article?

6. Why doesn't the church see herself as an army?

7. How may we stay dressed for battle?

8. How does busyness keep us from functioning as we should in the church?

9. How do you feel about the future of your congregation? Why?

10. How may we restore our biblical identity and mission?

5

Identifying the Enemy

When I was in Navy boot camp, we had several classes on how to identify enemy aircraft, ships, and actions. Our instructor said, "You can't combat the enemy if you can't identify him." When I was in the Police Academy we had classes on how to identify illegal drugs, suspicious behavior, and other actions of people. When I was doing graduate work in counseling, we learned how to profile various issues and diagnose solutions. Since September 11, 2001, America has escalated efforts to identify potential enemies. While all these efforts to identify enemies of society and our country are important in a physical sense, our real concern should be about enemies who seek to undermine and destroy the faith of Christians who are in the Lord's army.

If a soldier or sailor falls asleep on his post, he will be court martialed. Sleeping while on duty is a serious threat to security. As soldiers of Christ, we have a spiritual duty to stay awake and be vigilant with regard to watching for our enemy. That is why Paul warned, "Awake, you who sleep." And Peter warned, "Be sober, be vigilant; because your adversary the devil walks about like a roaring lion, seeking whom he may devour" (1 Peter 5:8).

Enemies Are Ever-Present

We need to wake up to the fact that Christians are promised there will be enemies. These enemies will be varied and from, in some cases, unsuspected sources:

1. *Jesus said our enemies may be in our own house:* "For I have come to 'set a man against his father, a daughter against her mother, and a daughter-in-law against her mother-in-law'; and 'a man's enemies will be those of his own household'" (Matthew 10:35–36).

2. *Paul promised that those who put God first will suffer persecution:* "Yes, and all who desire to live godly in Christ Jesus will suffer persecution" (2 Timothy 3:12). Notice Paul didn't say those "who were" living godly but those who "desire" to live godly.

3. *On the day of Pentecost, Peter preached from prophecy* that Jesus would be the one who would "make Your enemies Your footstool" (Acts 2:35).

4. *In His discourse on the parable of the sower, Jesus said this about one of the soils that didn't produce fruit:* "Yet he has no root in himself, but endures only for a while. For when tribulation or persecution arises because of the word, immediately he stumbles" (Matthew 13:21).

5. *Before his conversion, Saul was an enemy of the church:* "Now Saul was consenting to his death. At that time a great persecution arose against the church which was at Jerusalem; and they were scattered throughout the regions of Judea and Samaria, except the apostles" (Acts 8:1).

6. *Paul and Silas were put in prison for their faith:* "And when they had laid many stripes on them, they threw them into prison, commanding the jailer to keep them securely. Having received such a charge, he put them into the inner prison and fastened their feet in the stocks" (Acts 16:23–24).

7. *The apostle John was in prison on the Isle of Patmos:* "I, John, both your brother and companion in the tribulation and kingdom and patience of Jesus Christ, was on the island that is called Patmos for the word of God and for the testimony of Jesus Christ" (Revelation 1:9).

The church has not been free from enemies since it was established almost two thousand years ago. However, throughout all these centuries these enemies have taken on new names and faces and have attacked the followers of Christ in new ways. While we must not become paranoid, we must be awake to the reality of our enemies. We must recognize them, even in their new garments and new rhetoric. In his second epistle the apostle Peter warns us that enemies (false teachers) will "slip in the side door" and try to lead away "the elect of God." Read the entire book of 2 Peter for the full impact of this observation.

Postmodernism and Christianity

What is postmodernism? One older Christian brother said, "I may not know what postmodernism is but I know it ain't in my Bible." True, but that still doesn't help us realize how subtle and deadly that philosophy is to Christianity.

The word *postmodernism* literally means "after the modernist movement." While the word *modern* means "that which is related to the present," referring to the movement of modernism and the following reaction of postmodernism are defined by a set of perspectives. The word is used in critical theory to refer to a point of departure from works of literature, drama, architecture, cinema, and design, as well as in marketing and business and the interpretation of history, law, culture, and religion in the late twentieth century.

Postmodernism is issuing numerous challenges to long-held fundamental beliefs and interpretations of God's holy word, the Bible. Maybe we can illustrate this point.

A lady came into the preacher's office for counseling related to a relationship she was having with a man. After spending some time discussing her love and commitment to the man, the preacher asked, "But aren't you married?" The woman replied, "Yes, I am married." In a kind but firm voice the preacher replied, "You are committing adultery, which, according to the Bible, is a sin." Sitting up in her chair the woman quickly replied, "No I am not! That's just your opinion!" Then she quickly left the office.

In the mind of the woman, "opinion" was the same as "interpretation"; and "interpretation" was the same as "opinion." Her opinion (interpretation) was as valid as the preacher's. How does someone who professes to believe in the Bible reach the point of saying that "thou shall not commit adultery" is only a matter of opinion? Such thinking is an expression of the influence of postmodernism.

Postmodernism seeks to do away with the things religious people regard as essential; they believe every society is in a state of constant change; there are no absolute values or truths, only relative ones. This promotes the value of personal feeling and "religious impulses," which weakens the strength of "religions," such as Christianity, that claim to deal with a Higher Power called God and truths presented from "outside" sources such as revelation (the Bible).

In the world of postmodernism there are no universal religious or ethical laws, everything is shaped by the cultural context of a particular time and place in a community or society. A joke among postmodernist is, "The theology of the neighborhood bar is as valid as that of the clergyman."

"Just do what you feel or think is right" is not a new philosophy or belief system. The nation of Israel practiced this belief, "In those days there was no king in Israel; everyone did what was right in his own eyes" (Judges 17:6; cf. 21:25).

Postmodernism can be defeated only by going back to the ancient teachings of God's word. That requires teaching those subjects and doctrines that refute such enemies of the cross. Read Romans 1:18–32 to see the end result of leaving God out of your thinking and life.

Atheism and Christianity

The psalmist declared, "The fool has said in his heart, 'There is no God'" (Psalm 14:1). Throughout history there have always been those who chose to be atheists. Most mainstream believers in Christ have not looked on atheism as a serious threat to their faith. The major reason is that most atheists have been somewhat shy about declaring their atheism because of the rejection from society. That is rapidly changing.

Richard Dawkins, author of *The God Delusion* and one of the most recognized atheists in our day, is calling for his fellow atheists to "come out of the closet" and let their voices be heard. In a 2005 AP/Ipsos poll on religion, only two percent of Americans who responded said they did not believe in God, but Dawkins believes that is only because the majority remains "in the closet." Dawkins is on a campaign encouraging atheists to lift their voices against the "intrusion of religion in our schools and politics" and to express how tired they are of being "bullied by those who would force their own religious agenda down the throats of our children and our respective governments."

Atheism is on a crusade to:

1. Remove the Ten Commandments from all public buildings and government-owned or government-sponsored parks and facilities.

2. Remove prayer from all school sporting events—all school functions.

3. Remove tax-exemption for religious organizations such as churches and synagogues.

4. Deny freedom of speech for religious messages.

5. Control the content of the media to exclude religious expressions.

6. Forbid the mention of God or the supernatural from our moral principles and public policies.

Other best selling books such as *God Is Not Great: How Religion Poisons Everything*, by Hitchens, and *The End of Faith*, by Sam Harris, reflect the zeal in atheist critique of there is no God. Add to this list other books such as *The Da Vinci Code*, by Dan Brown, a national best seller, and you have a broader picture of how Satan is going all out with his agenda to destroy belief in God.

We can no longer sit comfortably in our pews singing "Soldiers of Christ, Arise." Regardless of how many people are atheists or whether or not they have formed a conspiracy,

Christians need to wake up and fight back with the sword of the Spirit.

Be Ready to Defend

Anthony Horvath, a former atheist and school teacher, has pointed out that many churches are not doing enough to counter the atheists' message, despite the truth that they possess (John 8:32, 36). Some churches, he thinks, are actually producing atheists by not explaining the basis of a Christian's faith in God's revelation, the Bible.

In *The Historicity of Jesus*, from the Atheist Foundation of Australia, there is a claim that the man Jesus, also known as the historic Jesus, never existed. They taunt the evidences used by Christians to verify the existence of Jesus as mainly coming from four sources: prophesies in the Old Testament, the four Gospels, the New Testament epistles, and the writings of non-Christians of the period. They taunt further that all these sources are tainted by inconsistencies, forgery, fraud, and lies by Christians who knew there was only scant evidence of the historical Jesus and who, therefore, attempted to create acceptable evidence. They also say that the virgin birth of Jesus was a hoax patterned after the birth of Horus to Isis, and the gods of both the Egyptians and the Romans, as well as others, before Christ was born. Wake up! Atheism is trying to get rid of Jesus; the only name under heaven whereby men can be saved (cf. Acts 4:11–13).

Most atheists believe it takes courage to be an atheist:

> Not one man in ten thousand
> has the goodness of heart
> or strength of mind
> to be an atheist.
> —Samuel Taylor Coleridge to Thomas Allsop, 1820

Not only do we need in-depth classes in the Bible to learn God's holy word, but we also need classes in Christian evidences, apologetics, world religions, and related fields to strengthen our faith in God and His word. Remember these words by Peter:

But sanctify the Lord God in your hearts, and always be ready to give a defense to everyone who asks you a reason for the hope that is in you, with meekness and fear (1 Peter 3:15).

Humanism and Christianity

Another enemy at the door of the church—even inside some—is humanism. What is humanism? The *thinkhumanism* website gives the following definition:

Humanism today can be described as a philosophy, a world view or life stance that focuses on the natural and human and rejects the supernatural. Humanism is positive, ethical, and democratic. It is underpinned by a commitment to rational enquiry and scientific method . . . Humanists accept that this is the only life we can know we have and that it is up to us to try to live it to the full . . . Humanists agree that human nature and experience are the only sources of morality . . . Humanists embrace the moral principle known as the Golden Rule . . . Humanism is not a faith position, although it is sometimes described as such by religious believers. Faith implies a belief without testable evidence. An absence of belief in gods or the supernatural is not a faith . . . faith is based on our knowledge of what humankind has already achieved (11-5-09).

In his book, *Humanism: An Introduction*, author Jim Herrick wrote,

Humanism is a most human philosophy of life. Its emphasis is on the human, the here-and-now, the humane. It is not a religion and it has no formal creed, though humanists have beliefs. Humanists are atheists or agnostics and do not expect an afterlife. It is essential to humanism that it brings values and meanings into life.

Robert G. Ingersoll (1833–1899), American political leader, said, "As people become more intelligent they care less for preachers and more for teachers" (cf. Romans 10:9–17). Ingersoll also said,

Reason, Observation, and Experience—the Holy Trinity of Science—have taught us that happiness is the only good. The place to be happy is here. The time to be happy is now. The way to be happy is to make others so.

Obviously, humanism is just another attempt to do away with Christianity as we biblically know it. It places human reasoning and experience at the apex of what is acceptable as long as you practice some form of the Golden Rule.

While secular humanists do not claim to be a religion or church, they have a set of common values or beliefs that bind them together. Their beliefs may be summarized as follows:

1. *Humanists champion tolerance and freedom.* Control and tyranny over the mind of man must be abolished; free enquiry must be allowed; all points of view must be heard; morals must not be imposed; thus, the absolute separation of church and state.

2. *Humanists embrace reason, not extra divine revelation.* The universe is all that exists or is real. Through human intelligence rather than in divine guidance, one comes to a more rational understanding of the world.

3. *Humanists believe a person can be moral, ethical, and honest without being committed to religion.* Children should be taught moral principles but not indoctrinated.

4. *Humanists place an emphasis on seeking knowledge,* trusting human wisdom, value, and celebrating arts, music, and literature—rather than seeking and valuing a God who does not even exist.

5. *Humanists believe in taking responsibility in the now;* don't wait for an imaginary deity to help or save you—take action; decide your own destiny. You can reason and think your way out of most problems.

6. *Humanists are altruistic, always seeking the greater good for humanity;* to always be socially and globally responsible and compassionate. Save the planet.

7. *Humanists do not believe in an afterlife.* They say there is no evidence that man has a "separate soul" or that any part of a person exists after physical death. Immortality is an illusion.

Major contributors to secular humanism include Aristotle, Epicurus, Voltaire, Hume, Thomas Paine, Charles Darwin, Robert Ingersoll, Corliss Lamont, and Paul Kurtz.

Most major universities and colleges in America have humanists on their faculty. Humanists are even teaching at elementary and high school levels. Humanism has found its way into some liberal theological seminaries and graduate schools of religion, so it is making inroads into churches via pulpits and leadership.

Christians, wake up to the enemy of humanism!

We have noted the need to identify enemies of the cross, but merely to identify them is not enough. We must put on the whole armor of God and fight the good fight of faith. We must not be deceived by leaders in and out of the church who are saying, "All is well and there is no need to be alarmed." There are wolves, both in and out of Christianity, dressed in sheep's clothing. A closed mind will be taken down the tubes by those who have a hidden agenda. It's time for Christians to wake up!

For Thought and Discussion

1. Why should we wake up to the enemies of the faith?

2. Why have we dropped our guard since 9/11?

3. What is the biggest enemy of Christianity today?

4. What is postmodernism? Why is it a threat?

5. Have you ever discussed Christ with an atheist?

6. Why are atheists becoming more aggressive?

7. What is humanism?

8. How is humanism making inroads into society and Christianity?

9. What are some subjects and classes you would suggest to develop for combating these enemies?

10. What additional observations do you have?

11. How do you plan to wake up to these enemies and fight them?

6

The God of Wake-Up Calls

Does it matter who wakes you up? Does it matter how someone wakes you up? Does it matter when someone wakes you up? The answer to these three questions is obvious—yes!

While we may not like being roused out of sleep, it does matter how we wake up. I have always thought the term "alarm clock" gets us off on the wrong foot. I like the term "opportunity clock." Why? Because "this is the day the Lord has made; we will rejoice and be glad in it" (Psalm 118:24). Today is a new opportunity to glorify God.

When my children were small, I returned to their rooms after first giving them the gentle wake-up call, creating the sound of a boatswain's pipe and loudly saying, "Reveille! Reveille! Up all mid-watch standers." To this day they still frown at the thought of those wake-up calls, especially when they hear me sounding them to my grandchildren. Some things never change.

When we give a wake-up call, we are in great company. From the moment God asked Adam in the Garden of Eden, "Where are you?" (Genesis 3:9), the Bible is filled with God's wake-up calls. Like a kind parent who gently, at first, shakes his children in an attempt to wake them, God gently shakes His children in an attempt to wake them from slumber. And if the gentle attempt doesn't work, the wake-up attempt becomes firmer and more serious. God is the Master of wake-up calls.

Examples of God's Wake-Up Calls

Let's take a few minutes and note some of God's wake-up calls. Since the Old Testament was written for our learning

(Romans 15:4), what do we learn about God's wake-up calls? The lessons are numerous.

As previously noted, God's first wake-up call was to Adam. After he and Eve violated God's positive divine law and ate of the tree of the knowledge of good and evil, they shamefully hid themselves (Genesis 3:8). God knew where they we hiding and issued a wake-up call. He always knows where people are hiding.

In the days of *Noah,* the world had become so corrupt that God planned to destroy it (Genesis 6). During all those years Noah was building the ark, he was also preaching. Peter says, God did not spare the ancient world "but saved Noah, one of eight people, a preacher of righteousness, bringing in the flood on the world of the ungodly" (2 Peter 2:5; cf. 1 Peter 3:19–20). God has always tried to wake people up to their sinfulness and coming judgment.

Another interesting wake-up call was at the *tower of Babel.* In a conspiracy made possible by everyone's speaking the same language, people came from all over and gathered on a plain in the land of Shinar (Genesis 11:1–2). Their goal was to build a city and a tower that reached into the heavens (Genesis 11:3–4). You, no doubt, know the rest of the story. God came down and not only confronted them but also gave them a wake-up call by confusing their language (Genesis 11:5–7). Cooperation was no longer possible, so they were scattered. God has all kinds of ways to wake people up.

Few wake-up calls in the Old Testament are as dynamic as the one issued by *Moses to the Pharaoh of Egypt.* Prior to his mission, Moses was given a wake-up call by God in the form of a burning bush (Exodus 3:1–7). After arguing with God, Moses went to Egypt equipped with one sermon which he preached ten times. It was titled, "Let My People Go!" Along with the ten sermons, Moses performed miracles that struck at the impotency of the idolatrous gods in Egypt. Each presentation was designed to wake Pharaoh so he would let God's people go. One by one he rejected God's wake-up calls. His eyes were finally opened when God killed all the firstborn of Egypt (cf. Exodus 12). But even after seeing the power of God demonstrated against his gods, he reverted to his old self. He hopped into his chariot and, along with his army, pursued God's people (Exodus 14). Because Pharaoh didn't heed God's wake-up call, his whole army was drowned in the Red Sea (Exodus 14:28–31). Serious consequences always occur when men ignore God's wake-up calls.

The *book of Judges* is a running account of God, time after time, through Judges 15, sounding wake-up calls. The cycle continued time after time: the people sinned, went into bondage, cried out, and God delivered them. If we learn anything from the Old Testament, it is that God's people have never stayed very faithful to Him for very long, and that they never once and for all took heed to His wake-up calls.

The *period of the kings* followed the same pattern we found in Judges. The nation rejected God as their king. They wanted a visible king like the heathen nations around them. So God gave them kings, the first being Saul. A reading of the books of Samuel, Kings, and Chronicles reveals God's patience and longsuffering with Israel by giving them one wake-up call after another.

Even after the fall of the united kingdom, God continued to call prophets to take His messages to His chosen people, Israel. God gave an interesting wake-up call through *Isaiah* to Jerusalem:

> Awake, awake! Put on your strength, O Zion; put on your beautiful garments, O Jerusalem, the holy city! For the uncircumcised and the unclean shall no longer come to you. Shake yourself from the dust, arise; sit down, O Jerusalem! Loose yourself from the bonds of your neck, O captive daughter of Zion! (Isaiah 52:1–2).

As God's spokesman, Isaiah's summon to Zion is like that of a drill sergeant as he calls them to wake up and dress themselves in all their strength and glory that honors Jerusalem, the city of the Holy One. Wake up! The days of captivity are over. Start acting like the people you are: God's chosen!

How about *Amos*, the tree-climbing prophet? He came from among the herds and trees to issue a clarion wake-up call to God's people. "Woe to you who are at ease in Zion, and trust in Mount Samaria, notable persons in the chief nation, to whom the house of Israel comes!" (Amos 6:1).

Prior to this wake-up call, God had said through Amos, "'Therefore I will send you into captivity beyond Damascus,' says the Lord, whose name is the God of hosts" (Amos 5:27). Sometimes the wake-up call is to announce that it's too late, judgment is coming; get ready.

Not all of God's wake-up calls in the Old Testament were to His people. The *book of Jonah* is a perfect example of how God sent His prophet Jonah to Nineveh, a very wicked city (Jonah 1:2). Most of us know how Jonah refused to take God's wake-up call to the wicked city. After three days in the large fish's stomach, Jonah got the missionary spirit. In his smelly clothes and fish oil all over his body, the reluctant prophet hit the streets of Nineveh preaching repentance. To Jonah's disgust, the Ninevites heeded God's wake-up call and repented (Jonah 3–4). You never know when people will wake up, so sound the alarm and patiently wait and see.

Moving on to the New Testament, we find a number of wake-up calls from God. The first one we note is *John the Baptist.* Malachi had predicted more than four hundred years before John came on the scene that one would come in the spirit of Elijah (Malachi 4:4–6).

What a sight! What a wake-up call from God's chosen messenger. "In those days John the Baptist came preaching in the wilderness of Judea, and saying, 'Repent, for the kingdom of heaven is at hand!'" (Matthew 3:1–2). John's preaching was a wake-up call to Israel that the Messiah they had been waiting for had arrived. But sadly, they refused to wake up. They kept snoozing in the traditions and rituals of the scribes and Pharisees (cf. Matthew 23). John announced in his Gospel, "He came unto His own, and His own did not receive Him" (John 1:11).

The *apostle Paul,* who had received a wake-up call from Christ (Acts 9), issued wake-up calls to churches. To the Romans he wrote:

> And do this, knowing the time, that now it is high time to awake out of sleep; for now our salvation is nearer than when we first believed. The night is far spent, the day is at hand. Therefore let us cast off the works of darkness, and let us put on the armor of light. Let us walk properly, as in the day, not in revelry and drunkenness, not in lewdness and lust, not in

strife and envy. But put on the Lord Jesus Christ, and make no provision for the flesh, to fulfill its lusts (Romans 13:11–14).

To the *Ephesians,* Paul wrote: "Therefore He says: 'Awake, you who sleep, arise from the dead, and Christ will give you light.' See that you walk circumspectly, not as fools but as wise" (Ephesians 5:14–15). In time that church fell asleep, left its first love, and ceased to exist. Regardless of the source, a wake-up call can be forgotten in time.

Because of their abuse of the Lord's supper, Paul wrote a wake-up call to the church in Corinth. In fact, many had already fallen asleep, spiritually speaking:

> For he who eats and drinks in an unworthy manner eats and drinks judgment to himself, not discerning the Lord's body. For this reason many are weak and sick among you, and many sleep (1 Corinthians 11:29–30).

Of course, Jesus Christ Himself issued many wake-up calls. After His victory over Satan in the wilderness temptations (Matthew 4:1–16), Jesus set His face toward the cross with a wake-up call to repentance: "From that time Jesus began to preach and say, 'Repent, for the kingdom of heaven is at hand' " (Matthew 4:17). In His great transitional sermon, the Sermon on the Mount (Matthew 5–7), Jesus tried to wake up Israel for a change from the Law of Moses to His law, the law of grace. They stayed asleep, and Paul wrote, "But their minds were blinded. For until this day the same veil remains unlifted in the reading of the Old Testament, because the veil is taken away in Christ" (2 Corinthians 3:14).

We have taken a brief look at some of the wake-up calls God has issued. It is clear that God is the God of wake-up calls. Some of these were direct, some through selected spokespersons, and some through the written word.

We have also noted that while God issued wake-up calls, many were ignored or observed for a short time. This is why we must continually listen to His wake-up calls in the word. God doesn't speak to us today in an audible manner; He speaks to us through His inspired word. It is powerful:

> For the word of God is living and powerful, and sharper than any two-edged sword, piercing even to the division of soul and

spirit, and of joints and marrow, and is a discerner of the thoughts and intents of the heart (Hebrews 4:12).

Every exposure to God's word, either by reading or listening to lessons and sermons, is a wake-up call. God is trying to get our attention. He wants us to turn off the snooze button, roll out of bed, and continue our fight of faith. Our Father is gently nudging us to wake up.

Christians, wake up!

For Thought and Discussion

1. Where was the first wake-up call given by God? Why?

2. Why does God bother to give wake-up calls?

3. What are some additional wake-up calls from God?

4. Why do people ignore God's wake-up calls?

5. Discuss a spiritual wake-up call you have had.

6. How can a Christian help wake up the church?

7. What are some signs that a congregation may need a wake-up call?

8. How does repentance relate to a wake-up call?

9. How do these proverbs relate to our study of wake-up calls? (Proverbs 6:9–10; 24:33).

10. What additional observations do you have about God's being a God of wake-up calls?

7

Ignorance Is Not Bliss

Centuries ago the prophet Hosea proclaimed this truth to God's people:

> My people are destroyed for lack of knowledge. Because you have rejected knowledge, I also will reject you from being priest for me; because you have forgotten the law of your God, I also will forget your children (Hosea 4:6).

Contrary to the old proverb that was popular when I was a boy, "ignorance is bliss," ignorance can be deadly. We need to wake up to the importance of knowing and applying God's word.

The definition of *ignorant* and *ignorance* from Webster's is:

> The condition of lacking knowledge or training; lacking knowledge or information about a particular subject or fact; uninformed, uneducated; unaware, unlearned; some synonyms are "illiterate or uneducated."

Is being uneducated, unlearned, and without training bliss? Is lacking certain vital knowledge bliss? Is being unaware of something eternally important bliss? Is being uninformed really bliss? I say no!

In his discourse to the Athenian philosophers, Paul said, "Truly, these times of ignorance God overlooked, but now commands all men everywhere to repent" (Acts 17:30).

The ostrich complex has no place in a Christian's life. Burying one's head in the sand and hoping things will go away or get better is contrary to the call to be watchful, to be on guard.

We need to wake up and obey the Proverbs writer's injunction to "buy the truth, and do not sell it" (Proverbs 23:23).

Why? Only the truth can free us (John 8:32); a lie has never set anyone free.

Decline in Bible Knowledge

There was a time when we were known as "book, chapter, and verse" people. It was said of some of our preachers that if the Bible were lost, they could restore it by quoting it from memory. Those days are merely notes in our history. The church is in a dumbing-down mode. There is a decline in basic Bible knowledge. For example, 30 years ago I would assign the students in my preacher training classes 15 portions of Scripture; three other teachers in the same quarter would assign approximately that same number of verses. A student in 10 weeks would memorize between 50 and 60 portions of Scripture. In some classes if the student memorized the book of the Bible we were covering in the course, he was exempted from the final examination. That has changed. Memorization of Scripture has gone the way of the 8-track tape player, the VCR, and other outdated items. Some students now moan and groan if they have to memorize five verses of Scripture.

When I first started to preach, congregations would ask prospective preachers questions about biblical beliefs and also about certain skills, one of which was, "Can you lead a pew packers' class?" The pew packers' class was conducted one hour before Sunday evening services. In the class, children assembled and engaged in Bible drills. The class leaders would ask questions like, "How many books are in the Bible?" The students would reply in chorus, "Sixty-six." During the course of a year, students would learn as many as two thousand facts from the Bible. Once-thriving Bible Bowls have ceased to exist in many congregations and sections of the country.

A cartoon depicted two older men leaving church services. One said to the other, "Have you noticed how things have changed in church?"

"What do you mean?" the other man asked.

"Well, when we used to come to church, we brought our Bibles. Now we need to bring our dictionaries."

In case you haven't noticed, there is a decline in exposure to God's word in the home, pulpit, and church classrooms. Pop psychology and feel-good, meet-my-needs messages have been substituted for a "thus saith the Lord." The command to "preach the word" is a relic of a bygone day.

In a Web article from *Christianity Today* (11-9-09), Mark Galli wrote a sobering article entitled "Yawning at the Word." His subtitle was "It's Really Hard to Listen to God Where There Are Really Interesting Things to Think About." In his articles he shares how a staff member told him he was using too many Scriptures in his sermons—from two to six verses. The staff member had said, "You'll lose people." The author asks this question: "Why have we become so impatient and bored with God's word?"

Jesus made it clear that only the truth would free people from sin (John 8:32). He also made it clear as to what consti-tutes the truth, "Sanctify them by Your truth. Your word is truth" (John 17:17).

Why this decline in Bible knowledge? There are several reasons:

1. A major emphasis on learning the word no longer exists. We confuse "exposure" to the word with learning the word.

2. Many who teach and preach do not use very much of the word. Example is powerful.

3. Some schools that train preachers no longer have a ma-jor emphasis on "preaching the word."

4. The impression that a minimum amount of Bible knowl-edge such as "What must I do to be saved?" is all you need to know.

5. A failure to obey the command to grow in knowledge is a major cause of Bible ignorance (cf. Hebrews 5:11–14; 2 Peter 1:5–11).

6. People are too busy to spend time studying the Bible. Some confuse reading the Bible with studying the Bible.

7. Many of our classes and sermons aren't designed or pre-sented in learning modes; they are more audit modes.

8. Leadership has not given the time, effort, and emphasis on becoming a learning church. Attendance is an end within itself.

9. Harboring secret sins will keep a Christian from studying and learning God's word as he should.

In your opinion what are some additional reasons for a decline in Bible knowledge:

1. _____

2. _____

3. _____

We need to wake up to the ignorance of God's word!

The Power of God's Word

In Genesis 1:3 we read, "Then God said, 'Let there be light'; and there was light." Time after time in the rest of chapter 1, we read, "Then God said." The word of God is powerful beyond our human comprehension. The Hebrews writer wrote,

> For the word of God is living and powerful, and sharper than any two-edged sword, piercing even to the division of soul and spirit, and of joints and marrow, and is a discerner of the thought and intents of the heart (Hebrews 4:12).

In his wake-up call to the Ephesians, Paul wrote this about the power of God's word: "And take the helmet of salvation, and the sword of the Spirit, which is the word of God" (Ephesians 6:17). The word is the tool to defeat the devil. When Satan tried to tempt Jesus, the Master replied, "It is written, 'Man shall not live by bread alone, but by every word that proceeds from the mouth of God'" (Matthew 4:4; Deuteronomy 8:3).

There is no chapter in the Bible that contains more praise and acceptance of God's word than Psalm 119. I have often thought that God should have required us to memorize it. Note a few of the praises of God's word in this magnificent chapter:

1. *Knowing God's word helps us obey God:* "When I learn Your righteous judgments, I will keep Your statutes" (119:7–8).

2. *Knowing God's word helps us cleanse our hearts:* "How can a young man cleanse his way? By taking heed according to Your word" (119:9).

3. *Knowing God's word can keep us from practicing sin:* "Your word I have hidden in my heart, that I might not sin against you" (119:11).

4. *Knowing God's word is a source of counseling:* "Your testimonies also are my delight and my counselors" (119:24).

5. *Knowing God's word provides comfort and strength:* "My soul melts from heaviness; strengthen me according to Your word" (119:28).

6. *Knowing God's word provides answers to those who challenge us:* "So shall I have an answer for him who reproaches me, for I trust in Your word" (119:42).

7. *Knowing God's word gives us hope:* "My soul faints for Your salvation, but I hope in Your word" (119:81).

8. *Knowing God's word will make us wise:* "You, through Your commandments, make me wiser than my enemies" (119:98).

9. *Knowing God's word gives us understanding and power to discern:* "Through Your precepts I get understanding; therefore I hate every false way" (119:104).

10. *Knowing God's word orders our steps:* "Direct my steps by Your word, and let no iniquity have dominion over me" (119:133).

11. *Knowing God's word is being able to know the entire truth:* "The entirety of Your word is truth, and every one of Your judgments endures forever" (119:160).

12. *Knowing God's word is a source of revival and renewal:* "Plead my cause and redeem me; revive me according to Your word" (119:154).

We have noted only 12 samples from the 176 verses in Psalm 119. We need to wake up to the power in this grand psalm. We need to read it, study it, meditate on it, and put it into practice in our daily lives.

For Thought and Discussion

1. How does Hosea 4:6–8 relate to a wake-up call?

2. How does Acts 17:30 relate to us today?

3. Why is there a decline in Bible study in most congregations?

4. Why don't some Christians want to study the Bible?

5. What is the value of knowing God's word?

6. How can we wake Christians up to the need for Bible study?

7. How has your Bible knowledge grown in the past five years?

8. How does knowing God's word empower us?

9. What additional observations do you have?

10. What one intentional thing will you do because of this lesson?

8

Wake Up:
It's Time for Inspection

When I was in the Navy there were several events that raised a sailor's stress level. One was the sound of General Quarters and Man Your Battle Stations. Another stressful event was the inspection of living quarters and work areas. Some of these inspections were announced: inspection time and what would be inspected. Others were unannounced, so we had to be prepared at all times. Those inspections were continual wake-up calls to be ready at all times for the white-glove brigade.

As Christians, we need to wake up to the fact that Jesus, the head of the church and is continually inspecting His church on a congregational level. What if we really believed Jesus was perpetually inspecting our congregation? Would our attitude and behavior be any different from the way it is now? My guess is yes.

Back to the Navy inspection story. The inspectors looked for different things during various inspections. Sometimes they inspected lockers, at other times the cleanliness of quarters, and sometimes the showers and toilets. The challenge was be prepared at all times; a carryover from my Boy Scout days— be prepared!

Wake up. It is inspection time. We have already noted that God is the God of wake-up calls. Therefore, we are not surprised to see His Son, Jesus Christ, giving wake-up calls to churches.

A dynamic biblical account of Jesus' wake-up call to churches is found in Revelation chapters 2 and 3: the seven churches of Asia. Jesus inspected these churches. Let's take a brief look at the inspections and the results of each. Wake up! Five of the seven churches were in trouble and needed wake-up calls to get back on track.

1. *The church in Ephesus.* We have more information about this church than any other in the New Testament. The church was established by the preaching and teaching of Paul, along with Priscilla and Aquila, fellow workers (Acts 18:18–21). Paul later returned to Ephesus and taught in the synagogue for three months (Acts 19:8). He then taught in the school of Tyrannus for two years (Acts 19:9–10). Within a short time the church had elders (Acts 20:17). The apostle Paul wrote an epistle to that congregation. From what we know about that church, it should have been grounded in the faith and mission oriented, but something happened. When we get to Revelation 2:4, we read these words from the owner and inspector of the church: "Nevertheless I have this against you, that you have left your first love." Sadly, the Ephesian church didn't heed Jesus' wake-up call. It ceased to exist.

2. *The church in Pergamos.* The owner and inspector of the church issued a wake-up call: "But I have a few things against you, because you have those who hold the doctrine of Balaam, who taught Balak to put a tumbling block before the children of Israel, to eat things sacrificed to idols, and to commit sexual immorality" (Revelation 2:14). This church did not heed the wake-up call from Christ.

3. *The church in Thyatira.* The owner and inspector issued a wake-up call: "Nevertheless I have a few things against you, because you allow that woman Jezebel, who calls herself a prophetess, to teach and seduce My servants to commit sexual immorality and eat things sacrificed to idols" (Revelation 2:20). This is the third church in Asia that didn't heed the wake-up call from Christ.

4. *The church in Sardis.* This is the fourth church in Asia that Jesus inspected: "I know your works, that you have a name that you are alive, but you are dead. Be watchful, and strengthen the things which remain, that are ready to die, for I have not found your works perfect before God" (Revelation 3:1–2). Another wake-up call, another rejected wake-up call.

5. *The church of the Laodiceans.* By now we know what to expect from churches given wake-up calls by Jesus: "Because you say, 'I am rich, have become wealthy, and have need to nothing'—and do now know that your are wretched, miserable, poor, blind, and naked" (Revelation 3:17).

How ironic! The owner of the church inspected and gave advice on how to correct the failed points of the inspection, but the churches didn't listen. Is it any wonder that churches today are not heeding the teaching of Scripture, the plea of leadership, and voices of concerned members?

How Prepared Are We for Inspection?
Let's imagination for a few minutes that Jesus is coming to inspect our congregation. He has given us the date and time. Here are some soul-searching questions:

1. What would our initial reaction be to this awareness?
2. What would change in order to be ready for the inspection?
3. Why would we change anything we are doing?
4. If we didn't know the exact time of inspection, what would our readiness level be?
5. What is our biggest needs area as a church?

Jesus is always aware of the state of His church. No surprises would confront Him if He came today.

The Church's Responsibility
Christ did not establish His church so we can be "at ease in Zion" (Amos 6:1; cf. Matthew 16:17–18). Neither does God add members to the body so they can be on vacation (1 Corinthians

12:18). We are a covenant people with an ordained mission. We have a function and job to perform. This mission has a foundation on which we must build:

> For other foundations can anyone lay than that which is laid, which is Jesus Christ (1 Corinthians 3:11).

> These things I write to you, though I hope to come to you shortly; but if I am delayed, I write so that you may know how you ought to conduct yourself in the house of God, which is the church of the living God, the pillar and ground of the truth (1 Timothy 3:14–15).

Among the numerous things these verses mean for members of the local church, here are a few:

1. We build our lives and teachings on Jesus Christ.
2. The church has the responsibility of being the support of the truth.
3. Our daily behavior depends on how we are building on these two foundations: Christ and the word of God.

We can't be in the slumber, snooze, or sleeping mode and expect these responsibilities to be dynamics in our daily Christian lives. We must wake up to this fact and stay awake improving it.

Wake up! It's time for an inspection.

For Thought and Discussion

1. Why is Christ interested in what's going on in His church?

2. In what sense does Christ inspect the church today?

3. How does our self-inspection relate to His inspection?

4. Why didn't the five churches in Asia correct their problems?

5. How does a wake-up call relate to our foundations?

6. What additional observations do you have?

7. How do you plan to use this lesson in your life?

8. What can a congregation learn from this lesson?

CHAPTER

9

Wake Up:
It's Thinking Time

How much time do you spend thinking about what you think? I imagine you are like most of us; that is, you spend very little time deliberately thinking about what you think. This is not just a play on words. The Bible speaks of a rich man who invites guests to eat as much as they wish, but that is not what he really thinks, and "as he thinks in his heart, so is he" (Proverbs 23:7). That general principle of one's being what one thinks is universally true.

At the top of the list of our wake-up calls is the need to wake up to our responsibilities relative to our thinking. Our daily behavior relates to what I call the TAR factor:

> Thoughts
> Actions
> Results

Every success or failure we experience in life, in one way or another relates to these three dynamics:

> *Thoughts:* We first create a thought and reflect on it.
> *Actions:* Then we take action on that thought.
> *Results:* Finally, we put our thoughts into action for the
> intended results.

TAR can be a powerful formula for helping us to stay awake and do God's will.

Some have charged that the human family doesn't do any real, in-depth thinking during the day, and that if we do any thinking at all, it is either negative or superficial at best. Some have poked fun at Christianity by calling it a "mindless religion." Others have said, "You don't have to park your brains in order to become a Christian."

The Power of Mindset

"His mind is set in cement." "My mind is made up." Mindsets are very powerful. They are attitudes and actions that reveal who and what we are. Mindsets are caused by thinking. Our mindset determines how we function in life:

1. Mindset determines how we cope with the daily challenges of life.

2. Mindset determines how we act and react to others.

3. Mindset determines our emotional state.

4. Mindset determines the emphasis we give to learning.

5. Mindset limits our achievement if not changed.

6. Mindset determines our beliefs and practices.

7. Mindset determines our relation to justice, right, and wrong.

8. Mindset can cause us to reject God's will for our lives.

9. Mindset can make us happy or miserable.

10. Mindset can determine our destiny: heaven or hell.

This is only a beginning list; it goes on and on as mindset impacts every area of our lives—cause and effect.

The Bible is full of examples of how mindsets have impacted people for negative and positive consequences. Remember TAR? We see it exemplified in the following examples:

1. Eve had her mind set on listening to the voice of a serpent, believing it would be okay to become a god herself (cf. Genesis 3:1–19). We know the rest of the story.

2. Cain, the son of Adam and Eve, set his mind on anger and pride, and chose to kill his brother, Abel (Genesis 4:1–9).

3. Noah's generation was destroyed because of their evil mindset: "Then the Lord saw that the wickedness of man was great in the earth, and that every intent of the thoughts of his heart was only evil continually" (Genesis 6:5).

4. Achan took precious treasures from Jericho, even though God commanded Israel not to take any of the spoils when the city fell. Israel lost her next battle with the little city of Ai! Why? Because of Achan's mindset. In his confession he said: "When I saw among the spoils a beautiful Babylonian garment, two hundred shekels of silver, and a wedge of gold weighing fifty shekels, I coveted them and took them" (Joshua 7:21).

God's law of sowing and reaping has always been in place (Galatians 6:8–10). Mindset plays the catalysis role in sowing and reaping. Jeremiah wrote, "Hear, O earth! Behold, I will certainly bring calamity on this people—the fruit of their thoughts, because they have not heeded My words, nor My law, but rejected it" (Jeremiah 6:19). It's the TAR effect again.

On one occasion Jesus was being questioned about what defiles a person. Those asking the questions had the Law of Moses and perhaps the traditions of the Pharisees in mind. But Jesus took it beyond external compliance to rules. Before listing a number of evil and sinful actions, Jesus said, "For from within, out of the heart of men, proceed evil thoughts" (Mark 7:18–23). It is in the mindset (thinking) that men begin the sin process.

Changing Your Thinking

The Bible reveals very clearly that in order to be pleasing to God, a person must change his mind. This is the basic meaning of the word *repentance*. The Greek word *metanoia* that is translated repentance means "to have another mind" or "to change one's mind." Jesus taught those of His day to repent or perish (cf. Luke 13:3, 5). When the Jews asked on the day of Pentecost what they must do, Peter replied, "Repent and . . . be baptized" (Acts 2:38). Change your mind about the Messiah and God's will for your life. And three thousand did (Acts 2:39–41).

God not only commands us to change our thinking, He also gives us a thinking agenda:

> Finally, brethren, whatever things are true, whatever things are noble, whatever things are just, whatever things are pure, whatever things are lovely, whatever things are of good report, if there is any virtue and if there is anything praiseworthy—meditate on these things (Philippians 4:8).

Once we have the attitude of Christ (Philippians 2:4–9), we have the core of our new thinking agenda, remembering as a man "thinks in his heart, so is he" (Proverbs 23:7).

Where we are today on our Christian journey was determined by what we were thinking yesterday. Our lives tomorrow will be determined by what we are thinking today. This is why we must guard our hearts and minds. We soon utter and do what is in our minds.

Concerning the significance of thinking, Jim Wheeler wrote:

> If you keep thinking in the same old way, you'll arrive at the same old conclusions and leave behind a well-worn rut of business-as-usual decisions. Trains must go where the tracks lead; they cannot follow unplanned routes. Similarly, if you always think along the same tracks, you will probably arrive at the same destination. But if you use a helicopter for your journey, you will not be limited by "tracks" (Jim Wheeler, *The Power of Innovative Thinking* [Franklin Lakes, NJ: National Press Publications, 1998], p. 7).

In His defense before Agrippa, the apostle Paul shared all the atrocities he sanctioned and participated in against Christians before his conversion. Why did Paul do such terrible things? His answer, "Indeed, I myself *thought* I must do many things contrary to the name of Jesus of Nazareth" (Acts 26:9–19). We all know the story. On the road to Damascus, Saul of Tarsus had an encounter with Christ, changed his mind (repented), and later was baptized into Christ (Acts 22:16; cf. 2:38).

Thought Control

Christianity is a journey. It is a journey that begins with a changing of the mind (repentance). The journey is a daily act of continually converting our old habits, thoughts, and desires into the attitude and image of Christ (cf. Ephesians 4:11–16). We are trying to develop a lifestyle consistent with our new identify: "Therefore, if anyone is in Christ, he is a new creation; old things have passed away; behold, all things have become new" (2 Corinthians 5:17). The new man cannot be led by the old ways of thinking (Romans 12:1–2).

When you hear the words *thought control,* what comes to mind? Some think of the word *propaganda:* "the attempts by governments to influence the thinking and behavior of people." Others might think of *brainwashing* such as occurs with prisoners of war. I once heard that the first casualty of war is truth. Truth, according to Jesus, is the only thing that can set you free (John 8:32, 36). That is why Solomon said, "Buy the truth, and do not sell it" (Proverbs 23:23).

Whatever controls our thoughts controls our lives. Progress is made or hindered by our thoughts. Behavior changes must first take place in the thought processes of the mind. Carlyle wisely wrote,

> Today is not yesterday . . . We ourselves change . . . How then, can our works and thoughts, if they are always to be the fittest, continue always the same . . . Change, indeed, is painful, yet ever needful; and if memory have its force and worth, so also has hope.

God said it first; it is an immutable law: "As he thinks in his heart, so is he" (Proverbs 23:7). Two thousand years ago Epictetus said, "We are disturbed not by things, but by the views we take of them." God said it first! But through the centuries men have been discovering this truth in philosophy, psychology, medicine, business, and sports.

Choice of Attitude

Every day we are given a set of circumstances with which we must deal. How we deal with them depends on our thinking—our attitude. If conditions alone made a man, then all men would be the same when given the same conditions. It's one's attitude toward the circumstance. "Two men look out through prison bars; one sees mud the other see stars." It is not the circumstances that make the person but his decision toward the circumstance, which is based on his thinking. In his bestseller, *Man's Search for Meaning,* Dr. Viktor E. Frankl, who endured years of unspeakable horror in Nazi death camps, wrote how he was able to survive:

> In the concentration camp every circumstance conspires to make the prisoner lose his hold. What alone remains is "the last of human freedoms"—the ability to "choose one's attitude in a given set of circumstances" (New York, NY: Pocket Books, 1984, p. 12).

The choice of attitude will not happen automatically unless long hours of personal discipline have been given to thought control. Thought control begins with monitoring your thoughts. Here is Paul's advice on how to do this:

> For the weapons of our warfare are not carnal but mighty in God for pulling down strongholds, casting down arguments and every high thing that exalts itself against the knowledge of God, bringing every thought into captivity to the obedience of Christ (2 Corinthians 10:4–5).

I once heard a professor say that between thirty thousand and sixty thousand thoughts pop in and out of a person's head every day. That's a lot of thoughts. Thankfully, most of them are fleeting and are gone even before we give them our attention, but some linger. They stay in our awareness and become part of our decision-making process. In these verses the apostle Paul gives us some sage advice on how to practice thought control:

1. He reminds us that our battle is not physical but spiritual—a battle for our minds (Ephesians 6:12).

2. He affirms that there are strongholds in our lives which seek to keep us carnal—defenses against God's will for our lives (2 Corinthians 10:4).

3. He reminds us of the role our imagination plays in how we handle our thoughts. (Read Genesis 6:5–6.)

4. He states that there will be thoughts in our minds that seek to exalt what we want above what God wants (Colossians 3:2).

5. He teaches us that this imagining and thought process seeks to get us to do things contrary to the knowledge we have learned as Christians (Galatians 5:17).

6. He further implies that we must capture each thought as we would capture an enemy who was seeking to do us harm (2 Corinthians 10:5).

7. Then we must take this thought to Christ and ask Him if we can obey it. If He says yes, then we can do it; if He says no, we must not do it (Romans 6:16; Hebrews 5:8).

Capture Thoughts

Let's take a few minutes and see how this thought control process advocated by Paul can work in our daily lives. Let's suppose you are dealing with a person who continually belittles you, makes fun of you, and is a challenge to be around. Your dislike for him increases and you begin to devise a way of getting back at him. Hold that thought! Capture it and take it to Christ and see if He will approve your planned actions. Based on what He taught, He says no:

> You have heard that it was said, "You shall love your neighbor and hate your enemy." But I say to you, love your enemies, bless those who curse you, do good to those who hate you, and pray for those who spitefully use you and persecute you (Matthew 5:43–44).

Let's imagine another situation. A person or family is in need. Some have put them down and called them shiftless or lazy. You visit them and are moved by their condition. You wonder (think) about whether or not you should help them. You take this thought to Christ. He answers yes: "Give to him who asks you, and from him who wants to borrow from you do not turn away" (Matthew 5:42). Jesus said, "It is more blessed to give than to receive" (Acts 20:35).

This exercise could go on and on, and it does in our daily lives as we capture our thoughts and take them to Christ for

His approval or disapproval. He is the one who must control our thinking. We must seek to have His attitude in all things (Philippians 2:4–9). A few years back there was a fad in which the letters WWJD were used. This stood for: What Would Jesus Do? When considered sincerely, that is not a mere fad. It's at the core of capturing and bringing our thoughts to Christ for approval or disapproval.

We must wake up to the importance of our thinking in our daily lives as Christians. We must think biblically, which is to think spiritually.

Personal Quiz

Using a 1-to-5 scale, with 5 being excellent, take a few minutes and reflect on your thinking relative to the areas listed below:

_____ I think biblically about my family.

_____ I think biblically about my coworkers.

_____ I think biblically about strangers I meet.

_____ I think biblically about my spouse.

_____ I think biblically about my work in the church.

_____ I think biblically about my choices in life.

_____ I think biblically about happiness in life.

_____ I think biblically about my friends.

_____ I think biblically about entertainment.

_____ I think biblically about success and accomplishments.

_____ I think biblically about the lost outside of Christ.

_____ I think biblically about my stewardship and finances.

_____ I think biblically about my goals in life.

_____ I think biblically about my spiritual growth in Christ.

Every action, whether good or bad, starts in the mind, because all actions are tied to our thinking. If we expect to change our lives as God intends us to do, we must change our thinking. We must wake up to this reality. "Be very careful about what you think. Your thoughts run your life" (Proverbs 4:23 NCV). We must be daily renewed through the transforming of our minds (Romans 12:1–2). That is why the proper place for us to set our minds is on things above, not on things below (Colossians 3:1–2).

For Thought and Discussion

1. Why do we need a wake-up call relative to thinking?

2. What is an automatic thought?

3. How does Proverbs 23:7 relate to life?

4. How does talking to ourselves relate to attitude?

5. How does repentance relate to mind change?

6. How do thoughts cause negative or positive actions?

7. Share some additional facts about Dr. Frankl and attitude.

8. How do you practice thought capturing?

9. How do we practice catastrophizing thinking? What is it?

10. What additional observations do you have?

11. How do you plan to use this lesson as a wake-up call?

10

Wake Up:
Pursuing Spiritual Maturity
Part I

Has anyone ever said to you, "Oh, why don't you grow up"? Have you every heard "he needs to grow up" uttered about a person? A small boy stands in front of his grandpa with a smile on this face, and says, "Grandpa, ain't I growed big?" A physician has to tell the parents of a newly born son that their son will not grow up to be normal, because he has some birth defects.

These illustrations have one thing in common: We are all interested, in one way or another, in growth and maturity. Maturity is the goal of the Christian life. The apostle Paul wrote, "But, speaking the truth in love, may grow up in all things into Him who is the head—Christ" (Ephesians 4:15).

> . . . to the measure of the stature of the fullness of Christ; that we should no longer be children, tossed to and fro and carried about with every wind of doctrine, by the trickery of men (Ephesians 4:13–14).

I am six-foot-two. When my son was growing up, he continually measured himself to see if he was going to be as tall as me. I remember the day he reached six feet, then when he grew one more inch. He didn't quiet make six-two, just six-one. Our goal according to Paul is to grow up into the fullness (height) of Christ. We need to wake up to this truth.

Maturing Is a Process Requiring Time

Maturing physically, intellectually, and emotionally takes time. When I was studying graduate psychology, I was taught that a human being goes through nine stages of development. These ranged from neonatal (1 month) to old age or senium (65 or 70). Each stage the human organism passes through is different. Each stage has unique characteristics, impulses, needs, functions, and challenges that require developmental adaptation.

Why do you suppose God uses the metaphor of a human so frequently in His word? (cf. 1 Corinthians 12). Obviously it is to teach us spiritual lessons. We don't need a degree in medicine or psychology to understand the basic process of growth stages a human goes through. We all start as babies and grow into adulthood. Just as no one is physically born full grown, no one is born spiritually full grown.

In his letter to the Hebrew Christians, the writer challenges them to stay on course, not to neglect their great salvation (cf. Hebrews 2:1–3). He reminds them that they haven't used their time wisely relative to growing as God desires:

> For though by this time you ought to be teachers, you need someone to teach you again the first principles of the oracles of God; and you have come to need milk and not solid food (Hebrews 5:12).

The Hebrews writer goes on and ties spiritual skills to the time factor: "For everyone who partakes only of milk is unskilled in the word of righteousness, for he is a babe" (Hebrews 5:13). Just because a new convert is forty years old with a college education and a CEO job doesn't mean he is mature in spiritual matters. We all begin the journey into the fullness of Christ as spiritual babes; the new birth affirms this truth (cf. John 3:1–7).

We need to wake up to the fact that by reason of time we need to mature—grow up in Christ.

Consequences of Immaturity

A newspaper recently carried an account of an eight-year-old boy who drove his father's car into a neighbor's house. The boy said his father had been teaching him how to drive, so he thought it was time for him to try it on his own. A few lessons on how to drive, a little experience in dad's lap, and a desire to take the car for a spin don't mean that a boy is mature enough to drive. His immaturity cost his father money and a day in court.

The name Corinth is synonymous with church problems. You name it, they probably had it. The apostle Paul rebuked them for being carnal and not spiritual (1 Corinthians 3:1–3). Paul said it was not his fault; he had fed them with milk, trying to help them mature properly. It wasn't working. He had to write two letters to them, trying to get them back on the right growth track—the track to spiritual maturity.

It seems the major problem in Corinth was the out-of-balance emphasis the church was placing on one's speaking a language one had not studied. Among the gifts the Holy Spirit was giving, this one was considered the superior one: the whole body was a tongue. Paul argues in chapter 12 that this isn't true; all members are important and all gifts are of equal value.

Paul zeroes in on their childish behavior. After setting forth love as the greatest virtue a Christian can develop, he reminds them of what childishness is like: "When I was a child, I spoke as a child, I understood as a child, I thought as a child; but when I became a man, I put away childish things" (1 Corinthians 13:11). Childish behavior is manifested in Corinth by the following actions and attitudes:

1. Childish behavior creates division and contentions among members of the church (1 Corinthians 1:10–11).

2. Childish behavior is seen in the desire to follow men instead of Christ (1 Corinthians 1:12; 3:4–7).

3. Childish behavior is created by the "wisdom of men" (1 Corinthians 2:4–6).

4. Childish behavior is the product of "the carnal man" (1 Corinthians 2:13–3:1 KJV).

5. Childish behavior is evidenced by the diet of milk (1 Corinthians 3:2).

6. Childish behavior is manifested in being proud and puffed up (1 Corinthians 5:2).

7. Childish behavior is demonstrated in tolerating sin (1 Corinthians 5:1–13).

8. Childish behavior is the practice of not being able to solve church problems but taking them to courts of law (1 Corinthians 6:1–8).

9. Childish behavior is not being able to recognize that your body is the temple of the Holy Spirit (1 Corinthians 6:19–20).

10. Childish behavior is a failure to understand and practice the respect and love needed in a marriage (1 Corinthians 7:1–39).

11. Childish behavior is making an issue out of sacrifices offered to idols (1 Corinthians 8:1–13).

12. Childish behavior doesn't understand the work of God's servants (1 Corinthians 9:1–27).

13. Childish behavior doesn't understand the total implication of conversion and fellowship in the church (1 Corinthians 10:1–33).

14. Childish behavior is displayed in an abuse of the Lord's supper (1 Corinthians 11:20–35).

15. Childish behavior is manifested in pride, abuse, and exclusiveness relative to spiritual gifts (1 Corinthians 12:1–31; 14:1–40).

16. Childish behavior is the result of a failure to grow and develop in love—*agape* (1 Corinthians 13:1–13).

17. Childish behavior is the inability to understand and support the truth about the resurrection of the body (1 Corinthians 15:1–58).

18. Childish behavior is seen when rejecting and despising a minister of the gospel (1 Corinthians 16:10–11).

We need to wake up to the serious consequences of immaturity in every area of our lives, especially in our spiritual growth.

Gauging Spiritual Maturity

The apostle Paul wrote that the goal of his ministry, and of ours, was to help every Christian nature in Christ: "Him we preach, warning every man and teaching every man in all wisdom, that we may present every man perfect in Christ Jesus" (Colossians 1:28).

The word *perfect* as used in the King James Version means "complete, whole, and mature" and comes from the Greek word *teleios*. The New American Standard Bible translates it as "present every man complete in Christ." The Revised Standard Version translates it as "present every man mature in Christ."

Few things are more challenging in Christianity than trying to gauge spiritual maturity. The status of a congregation is gauged by its concept of spiritual maturity. If it is not biblical, the church will not grow and function properly. An understanding of what constitutes spiritual maturity starts with the leadership of the church. Their views and practices will shape the direction of the church.

Inaccurate Gauges of Spiritual Maturity

There are numerous gauges used by churches to affirm spiritual maturity. These markers provide goals for the members of the congregation. Speaking truthfully, many of these gauges aren't in harmony with the biblical definition of spiritual maturity. Here are some inaccurate gauges of spiritual maturity:

1. *The attendance gauge.* Merely attending church services doesn't prove, per se, the spiritual maturity of the attendee. Jesus told the church in Pergamos, "I know your works, and where you dwell, where Satan's throne is." (Revelation 2:13). Satan attends church so he may steal the word from the people's hearts (Luke 8:12). We must not minimize church attendance because it is required (cf. Hebrews 10:24–25). However, in and of itself, it is not

a true gauge of spiritual maturity. Some are in the assembly against their will or to be marked "present." Their showing up each week doesn't necessarily engage them in the ministry of the church.

2. *The verbal belief gauge.* Just because a person says he believes in God, this doesn't prove he is spiritually mature. The devil has faith: "You believe that there is one God. You do well. Even the demons believe—and tremble!" (James 2:19). What the lips say may not be the true picture of the heart. Jesus said, "Well did Isaiah prophesy of you hypocrites, as it is written: 'This people honors Me with their lips, but their heart is far from Me'" (Mark 7:6). Yes, it is imperative that we believe in God, but a mere verbalization of this belief is not enough. We must practice what we believe.

3. *The knowledge gauge.* Knowing the Bible is essential (John 8:32). Playing Bible trivia can be fun at a fellowship or home gathering. Bible Bowls are great opportunities to share God's word. We must study to show ourselves approved unto God (1 Timothy 2:15). Sadly, history and contemporary evidences show that some of the worst crimes have been committed by people who know the Bible. To win theological arguments brings satisfaction, but it doesn't prove that the winner is spiritually mature. Even Satan knows and quotes Scripture (cf. Matthew 4:1–11). One man said, "I have been believing the Bible for thirty years and practicing it for one year." The Bible places the emphasis on doing God's word, not just knowing it for the sake of knowing it (cf. James 1:21–25; Matthew 7:21–23).

4. *The frugality gauge.* Stewardship is a vital test of one's spiritual maturity. It has been estimated that twenty-five percent of Jesus' teaching related to material things. As stewards we must be faithful (1 Corinthians 4:2). Some congregations, however, pride themselves on meeting their small budgets each week. They pay their bills, keep workers' salaries small, and rarely launch out on new

mission projects or local works. The balance on the check-book determines what will be done for the Lord. Their faith is only as large as this balance. The leaders think they are doing God a favor by "saving" His money instead of using it for reaching the lost. The other extreme is seen in congregations that boast of their large budgets and use financial generosity as a gauge of spiritual maturity. This was the problem with the church in Laodicea (Revelation 3:14–22).

5. *The involvement gauge.* Thank God for the fifteen to twenty percent of church members who are actively involved in the various programs of the church. Busyness is a must for some members and church leaders as a test of spiritual maturity. One leader constantly quoted, "Busyness is next to godliness," as though it is in the Bible. I know of church work projects in which some participants not only had disagreements but also used foul language and made threats in displays of anger. That kind of behavior is not spiritual maturity.

6. *The sound doctrine gauge.* Most Bible students know that we must contend for the faith (Jude 3), and be ready always to give answers (1 Peter 3:15). We must hold fast to sound words (2 Timothy 1:13). Sometimes we forget that "sound" is a translation of the Greek word *hugiaino* and means "to be healthy, sound, without flaw." "Doctrine" is from the Greek word *didaskalia* and means "teaching." Teaching that is healthy—sound doctrine—is the truth spoken in love (Ephesians 4:15). It is not degrading, belittling, offensive, or fussing. Some leaders and followers are known for their firm stand for sound doctrine, but their attitudes are far from being Christlike (Philippians 2:4–9). They seem to delight in splitting churches, in most cases, over opinions rather than healthy teaching given by God.

7. *The leader gauge.* The Bible affirms that elders must be mature men, not novices in the faith (cf. 1 Timothy 3:1–7). Deacons must also be proven (1 Timothy 3:8–13),

preachers must be examples (1 Timothy 4:12), and teachers must be faithful (2 Timothy 2:1–3). These and other functions in the church are rightly called leadership roles. One may be called a leader and function in a capacity successfully, yet still not be spiritually mature. Jesus agrees: "Let them alone. They are blind leaders of the blind. And if the blind leads the blind, both will fall into a ditch" (Matthew 15:14). John writes about a leader named Diotrephes, who was anything but spiritually mature: "I wrote to the church, but Diotrephes, who loves to have the preeminence among them, does not receive us" (3 John 9–10).

8. *The age gauge.* With old age, wisdom and spiritual maturity should become a reality. God's word places a special emphasis on the place of honor for the older saint. In some congregations, the words and attitudes of some of the older members are taken above what the Bible actually says. Their opinions are all that matter. After all, they have been in the church for years and "fought all the battles." In some cases they are the financial backers of most projects and programs. Having gray hair, many birthdays, and dressing well doesn't prove spiritual maturity. Thank God for aged saints and their contribution to the kingdom's mission, but old age isn't a guarantee of spiritual maturity.

9. *The public gauge.* Some Christians are gifted with speaking and teaching ability. They are used as teachers and preachers. Having a loud voice and domineering personality in the pulpit or behind the teaching lectern doesn't prove that a person is spiritually mature. Being given the title "minister" or "preacher" doesn't automatically increase one's spiritual maturity. It is wonderful that some are able to take part in public ways in the church, but public participation is not proof of spiritual maturity.

10. *The linguistic gauge.* This gauge is used to affirm the spiritual maturity of those who always have something spiri-

tual to say in every situation: "Bless his heart" or "We need to pray for brother Doe." This behavior comes across as being excessively righteous and pious. It puts a "holy glow" or "halo affect" over the gracious person's head. Such persons say things that are deep, challenging, and inspiring, yet, in many cases, their hearts are far from God as were the Pharisees (cf. Matthew 23).

Many others can be added to those ten gauges. Keep in mind this list is not designed to question anyone's present status relative to their spiritual maturity. Each of us must honestly examine our hearts to see if any of these apply to our concepts of what constitutes spiritual maturity. This is a positive wake-up call for us to mature in Christ.

For Thought and Discussion

1. Why is maturity important?

2. What happens if a person doesn't develop physically?

3. Who is the most mature Christian you know? Why?

4. What immature actions have you seen among Christians?

5. Reflect on the immaturity of the church in Corinth.

6. What does *perfect* mean?

7. What hinders a person from maturing spiritually?

8. How have you matured spiritually over the years?

9. What additional observations do you have?

10. How do you plan to use this lesson?

11

Wake Up:
Pursuing Spiritual Maturity
Part II

In our last lesson we noted that the goal of teaching, preaching, and personal discipline is for the maturing of Christians: "Him we preach, warning every man and teaching every man in all wisdom, that we may present every man perfect in Christ Jesus" (Colossians 1:28).

"Paul, where are you taking the people to whom you minister?"

"I am taking them on the road to maturity—to Christ!"

Church leadership must answer this question: Where are you taking the people who are following you? The answer should be the same as Paul's: We are taking them on a road to maturity—ultimately to Christ. That is one of the reasons God has given us church leaders:

> And He Himself gave some to be apostles, some prophets, some evangelists, and some pastors and teachers, for the equipping of the saints for the work of ministry, for the edifying of the body of Christ (Ephesians 4:11–12).

What's the Target?

Can you imagine a platoon of soldiers walking out of the safety of their guarded fortress to engage some unknown target in some unknown place? Likewise, can you imagine jumping into your car and heading down the road with no idea of where you are going? Yet that's what many do as Christians.

They have experienced the new spiritual birth but they don't know their next appointment.

What is spiritual maturity? It's amazing how many Christians don't have a sound, confirmed Bible answer to that question. How can you grow spiritually if you don't know what spiritual maturity is?

A couple of years ago I heard the results of a survey taken among professing Christians. It was taken in August 2008 by the Barna Research Group for a group called Living on the Edge. The survey interviewed 1005 adults, 18 years and older, including 611 clergymen. Sadly, the survey pointed out that most churchgoers in America can't biblically define spiritual maturity. The survey discovered that an overwhelming 81 percent equated spiritual maturity with "trying hard to follow the rules described in the Bible." Shockingly only 30 percent believed having a personal relationship with Christ defines spiritual maturity. Fourteen percent said living a moral life constitutes spiritual maturity, 12 percent said applying the Bible to life situations, and 6 percent said sharing their faith was a demonstrating proof of spiritual maturity.

The survey revealed some interesting things about the mindset of preachers relative to spiritual maturity. While nine out of ten believed a lack of spiritual maturity was a problem in our nation, a minority believed a lack of spirituality was a problem in their churches. A major shocking revelation of the survey was the divergent views held by preachers relative to what constitutes spiritual maturity. The gauge of the spirituality of members included the practice of spiritual disciplines (19 percent), being involved in church activities (15 percent), teaching the gospel to others (15 percent), having a personal relationship with Jesus (14 percent), having a concern for others (14 percent), applying the Bible to life issues (12 percent), being willing to grow spiritually (12 percent), and knowledge of the Bible (9 percent). How can preachers and leaders who are so vague in defining spiritual maturity lead people to spiritual maturity?

Again, if we don't know what the target of spiritual maturity is, how can we move toward it? We can't! How can we impact the world with spirituality if we don't know what it is?

How can a church be all God intends if it doesn't know what spiritual maturity is?

Review the last lesson on what spiritual maturity is not.

Peter Pan Syndrome

We are all in the same boat as was the apostle Paul when he wrote to the Philippians. We have not arrived!

> Brethren, I do not count myself to have apprehended; but one thing I do, forgetting those things which are behind and reaching forward to those things which are ahead, I press toward the goal for the prize of the upward call of God in Christ Jesus. Therefore let us, as many as are mature, have this mind (Philippians 3:13–15).

Even though I haven't arrived relative to spiritual maturity in all areas of my life, I know one thing: we must want to grow spiritually before it will become a reality. Spiritual maturity starts with an attitude, an attitude that is Christlike (Philippians 2:4–9). Sadly, some Christians don't seem to want to mature spiritually. They have the Peter Pan syndrome.

The story of Peter Pan, written by J. M. Barrie, was first published in 1911. Wishing to escape the responsibilities of being an adult, Peter Pan was determined to stay eternally young and live carefree in *Never Never Land*. In this fictional work, Peter Pan teaches Wendy and her younger brothers how to fly, and then it's off to magical *Never Never Land* for adventures with mermaids, Indians, and wicked Captain Hook and his pirate crew. As a play the full title was *Peter Pan* or *The Boy Who Would Not Grow Up*.

When Michael Jackson was interviewed in 2003 by Martin Baslie, Jackson said, "I'm Peter Pan." Bashir replied, "No, you're Michael Jackson." Michael replied, "I'm Peter Pan in my heart."

Some Christians are Peter Pan in their hearts—they don't desire to grow up. Too many responsibilities.

The *Peter Pan Syndrome* is a pop psychology term coined by Dan Kiley in his book, *Peter Pan Syndrome: Men Who Have Never Grown Up.* It has become a metaphor for Christians who don't grow up. Spiritually speaking, there are numerous people who become children of God—babes in Christ—but never become spiritual adults. Chronological age has little to do with growing into spiritual maturity; spiritual age and development depends on attitude and doing of God's word (cf. James 1:22–25). "By reason of time . . ." (Hebrews 5:12–13 KJV).

Spiritual Maturity Is a Journey

Just as attaining physical maturity takes time, growing in spiritual maturity takes time. Remember these four points:

1. *The growth of the spiritual man is not automatic.* When you are born of water and the Spirit, you are raised to begin to walk in a new life. This is the beginning of a lifelong process called conversion. The Hebrews writer said God gives us time to grow. How much? I don't know!

2. *Spiritual growth is not the exclusive territory of a select few,* such as theologians, teachers, preachers, and "spiritual giants." Spiritual maturity is not possessed only by those who pray, fast, and read their Bibles every day. It is attainable by every child of God.

3. *Spiritual growth will not occur unless you want to grow more toward Christlikeness.* We rarely do anything we don't want to do. God desires that we have a want-to-grow attitude. Our goal must be: I want to grow up and be just like my "big brother," Jesus Christ (Ephesians 4:11–16).

4. *Just as your physical development may be arrested or stunted,* your spiritual growth may be arrested too. The key is to eat the right spiritual food and do the proper spiritual exercises.

Jesus said love is powerful; so much so that our obedience to His commandments is tied to our love for Him: "If you love me, keep My commandments" (John 14:15). In order to obey the greatest commandment, we must love God:

> And you shall love the Lord your God with all your heart, with all your soul, with all your mind, and will all your strength. This is the first commandment (Mark 12:30).

Love demonstrated among Christians is so powerful it will attract outsiders to know you have been with Jesus (cf. John 13:31–33).

We have noted Paul's teaching about mature love in contrast to immature love: Love is not self-seeking (1 Corinthians 13:5). Notice the contrast between selfish, self-seeking love and outward demonstrations of mature love as presented in 1 Corinthians 13. (Read the chapter from the New King James Version.)

Chapter	Immature Love	Mature love
1	Is short on patience	Suffers long
2	Is not kind	Is always kind
3	Is envious	Is never envious
4	Shows off	Does not parade self
5	Is very rude	Is never rude
6	Self-seeking	Is never self-seeking
7	Gets mad easily	Not easily provoked
8	Thinks the worst	Thinks no evil
9	Gloats over wrongs	Never rejoices in evil
10	Rejects truth	Rejoices in truth
11	Is short-fused	Bears all things
12	Always skeptical	Believes all things
13	Is pessimistic	Hopes all things
14	Gives up easily	Endures all things
15	Immature love fails	Never fails
16	Is inferior	Is the greatest
17	Don't pursue it	Pursue love (1 Cor. 14:1)

Notice the great gulf between immature love and mature love in the above chart. The journey from immature, self-seeking love to mature love is a long one. It can be crossed only with God's power and our commitment to be daily "doers of the word" (1 John 4:4; Ephesians 3:20; James 1:22–24). There is only one attitude that can cross this great gulf: the attitude of Christ (Philippians 2:4–9).

Where are you on your journey from immature love to mature love? Go back to the above list and draw an arrow from left to right—from immature to mature love—indicating where you are in your present journey to spiritual maturity. Here is an example:

Short temper > > > > > > > > > > > > > > > > > > > Suffers long

   0%   25%   50%   75%   100%

Remember: You and you alone, are responsible for how you proceed on your journey to spiritual maturity. A successful journey requires TAR: Right Thinking, Right Attitude, and Results will be the reward. Only you can choose to think and behave in a manner that will bring more spiritual maturity. Only you can tackle and fight off old negativity, carnality, blaming others, and circumstances for your stunted growth into Christlikeness. Remember the following points:

1. God has not commanded the impossible (John 14:15; Revelation 22:14).

2. We must use what God has given us (Luke 12:48).

3. The choice of attitude makes the difference (Philippians 2:4–9).

4. You are in control of who places limitations on you (1 John 4:4).

5. Remember to use TAR: Thoughts—Actions—Results.

6. You must embrace and manage change, or it will enslave and manage you.

7. Yes, "I can do all things through Christ, who strengthens me" (Philippians 4:13).

For Thought and Discussion

1. How has your thinking changed relative to spiritual maturity?

2. Why doesn't attending church automatically grow a Christian?

3. Why do some desire to stay immature?

4. Discuss the *Peter Pan Syndrome.*

5. What is your personal plan to grow spiritually?

6. What is the first step toward spiritual maturity?

7. What are some additional signs of immature love?

8. How did you rate on the love scale?

9. What additional observations do you have?

10. How do you plan to use this lesson?

12

Wake Up:
No More Excuses or Blaming

We live in an age of excuse making and blaming by people who try to avoid accepting responsibility for their actions. We need to wake up to this immature attitude and action. President Harry S. Truman put responsibility in perspective when he said these four words: "The buck stops here." However, few people, even in the church, want to take on a responsibility or be responsible for much of anything.

What is responsibility? An unofficial but workable definition is "respond with ability." Webster defines responsibility as "the state or fact of being responsible." He defines responsible as "answerable or accountable, as for something within one's own power, control, or management . . . involving accountability." These definitions are in harmony with what we see in the Bible.

God Assigns Responsibilities

Our greatest grandparents, Adam and Eve, were given responsibilities and held accountable for those responsibilities. We are in the predicament we are in today because they failed to maintain integrity relative to their responsibilities in the Garden of Eden. You know the story.

Adam and Eve where given the oversight of a beautiful garden. They could have anything in the garden except one thing. They were not to eat of the "tree of knowledge." To do so would bring death. What an amazing and honorable responsibility this first couple had. God never advocates freedom from responsibility; in fact, just the opposite. Most Sunday school children know the rest of the story. Satan appeared to Eve and she surrendered her responsibility and obeyed the evil one's voice. Adam followed her example.

Ashamed and hiding in the bushes because he is afraid—he has blown his responsibility—Adam hears the voice of God, "Where are you?" (Genesis 3:9). The consequences were severe: spiritual death, pains in giving birth, subjection to her husband, and being driven from the Garden of Eden and sentenced to hard labor (cf. Genesis 3:16–24). They exchanged an honorable responsibility for one of sorrow and heartache.

God always assigns responsibility.

Bible Examples: Responsibility

Noah was a responsible man. According to the apostle Peter, he was a preacher of righteousness. His contemporary world had reached the point of no return:

> Then the Lord saw that the wickedness of man was great in the earth, and that every intent of the thoughts of his heart was only evil continually . . . So the Lord said, "I will destroy man whom I have created from the face of the earth" (Genesis 6:5–7).

Imagine! Noah was given the responsibility of building an ark, a huge vessel he had never heard of, much less seen. What a long and demanding task! He fulfilled his responsibility: "Thus, Noah did; according to all that God commanded him, so he did" (Genesis 6:22). His responsibility didn't end with the building of the ark. He had to become a zoo keeper and select and take on board the proper number of all kinds of animals (cf. Genesis 7:1–17).

Then there was the aged couple, Abraham and Sarah, to whom God gave the responsibility of being the parents of a great nation. They were too old to have children, but when God assigns a responsibility, He provides the ways and means for its becoming a reality (cf. Genesis 12–17).

The Old Testament is full of accounts of how God assigned responsibilities to various persons. Some successfully fulfilled their responsibilities; others did not. There is always a choice when God assigns a responsibility: you can accept or reject the duty (cf. Joshua 24:15).

In the New Testament we read the account of Jesus assigning His apostles the responsibility of leading the church in preaching the gospel to the world (cf. Mark 16:15–16; Matthew 28:18–20). They faithfully carried out their responsibility. (Read the book of Acts; see also Colossians 1:28.) The church in the twenty-first century is still responsible for carrying on that assignment. The evidence, however, says we aren't doing a very effective job in fulfilling our responsibility. The world is still lost.

Are we, as a church and as individuals, aware of the responsibilities God has assigned us? If so, how are we fulfilling them? If not, why aren't we fulfilling them?

Responsibility Is a Stewardship Practice

Responsibility is not an arbitrary issue but one tied to stewardship. Webster defines *steward:*

> One who manages another's property or financial affairs; one who administers anything as the agent of another or others; one who has charge of the household of another; an employee who has charge.

Stewardship is a trust. God requires that stewards be faithful in carrying out their responsibilities:

> Let a man so consider us, as servants of Christ and stewards of the mysteries of God. Moreover it is required in stewards that one be found faithful (1 Corinthians 4:1–2).

Peter wrote, "As each one has received a gift, minister it to one another, as good stewards of the manifold grace of God" (1 Peter 4:10). From a biblical perspective responsibility is just another word for stewardship.

Jesus taught numerous lessons on stewardship. He left no doubt relative to the importance of being faithful to a responsibility once it has been assigned to you:

1. The Parable of the Faithful Servant (Luke 12:41–48).
2. The Parable of the Dishonest Servant (Luke 16:1–13).
3. The Rich Man and Lazarus (Luke 16:19–31).

Every Christian has been given a stewardship assignment over all the things committed to him by God. Therefore, we must exercise faithful care over the responsibilities assigned to us. This means that we must wake up to our awesome responsibility, as stewards in God's house (cf. 1 Timothy 3:15; Revelation 2:10).

Some of Our Responsibilities

As faithful stewards of the responsibilities God has assigned us, we must not only know what they are but be proficient in carrying them out: "To whom much has been committed, of him they will ask the more" (Luke 12:48). We have been given everything we need to live a faithful Christian life; to be productive in the kingdom of God (2 Peter 1:3). We have been given commandments that demand responsibility and accountability. This is eternally serious and demands a wake-up call every day.

Underline this truth: No other member in the body of Christ can fulfill my responsibilities. We may help each other fulfill responsibilities, but we can't assume them. This is the dynamic of the body metaphor Paul used in 1 Corinthians 12. Here are a few of these personal responsibilities we have as Christians:

1. *We have the responsibility to pray.* No one can relieve us of this responsibility (1 Thessalonians 5:17).

2. *We have the personal responsibility to worship God in spirit and in truth* (John 4:23–24). No one can do that for us.

3. *We have a personal responsibility to be a teacher* (Hebrews 5:12). No one can free us from that responsibility.

4. *We have the responsibility to be faithful unto death* (Revelation 2:10). No one can be faithful for us.

5. *We have the responsibility to give as we have prospered* (1 Corinthians 16:1–2). Someone else might drop it in the collection plate for me, but it must originate with me as my gift.

6. *We have the responsibility to attend the assembly* (Hebrews 10:24–25). No one can represent me at the supper table with the King each Sunday.

7. *We have the responsibility to share the gospel with others* (Matthew 28:18–20; 2 Corinthians 4:7). No one can replace me "in my world as I am going." I am assigned there with the gospel. Someone may assist me but no one can relieve me of my responsibility.

8. *We have the responsibility to sing and make melody in our hearts* (Ephesians 5:19; Colossians 3:16). Someone may sing along with me but not for me.

9. *We have the responsibility for being doers of the word* (James 1:22–24). No one can do God's word for me. I must do it myself.

10. *We have the responsibility to visit those in need* (James 1:27; Galatians 6:10). Others may go with me or help me, but it doesn't relieve me of my duty.

11. *We have the responsibility to produce the fruit of the Spirit in our lives* (Galatians 5:22–25). No one can produce it in my life for me. I am responsible.

12. *We have the responsibility for having the attitude of Christ* (Philippians 2:4–9). No one can have that attitude for me.

13. *We have the responsibility for walking in the light as Christ is in the light* (1 John 1:7). No one can walk in the light for me.

14. *We have the responsibility to love one another* (John 13:31–34). No one can love anyone else for me.

15. *We have a responsibility to study God's word* (John 8:32; 2 Timothy 2:15). I may study with someone but that person cannot relieve me of my responsibility.

16. *We have a responsibility to grow into maturity; into the fullness of Christ* (Ephesians 4:11–16). Others may help me but they can't grow for me.

17. *We have the responsibility for practicing God's thinking agenda* (Philippians 4:6–9). No one can do my thinking for me (Proverbs 23:7).

18. *We have the responsibility of glorifying God* (Ephesians 3:21). No one can glorify God for me.

19. *We have the responsibility for being holy as God is holy* (1 Peter 1:16; 2:9). Nobody can be holy for me. Holiness is my personal responsibility.

20. *We have the responsibility to be imitators of God* (1 Corinthians 11:1; Ephesians 5:1–5). No other member in the church can imitate God in my life.

21. *We have the responsibility to bear one another's burdens, to help one another* (Galatians 6:2).

There are more than thirty-five "one another" passages in the New Testament that bind on us additional responsibilities to care for each other. No one can relieve me of these "one another" responsibilities.

From the day of one's new spiritual birth to the day of dying faithful in Christ, the daily walk with Christ is one of responsibility. The challenge involves:

1. Being aware of each responsibility.
2. Understanding each responsibility.
3. Believing you are personally responsible.
4. Making a commitment to being responsible.
5. Taking action every day toward being responsible.
6. Evaluating results of responsibility behaviors.
7. Fighting the temptation to give up because of setbacks.

Accepting Responsibilities

It is one thing to accept God's gift of salvation through Christ and yet something else to accept the responsibilities that go with it. "Everybody wants a paycheck, but very few want to work." An old country song says, "Everybody wants to go to heaven, but nobody wants to die." Everybody wants the benefits in Christ, but nobody wants the responsibilities. "The great thought," wrote Giosue Borsi, "the great concern, the great anxiety of men is to restrict, as much as possible, the limits of the responsibility" (Source unknown).

We must accept responsibility for our attitudes, actions, and lives. Psychologist Albert Ellis wrote:

> The best years of your life are the ones in which you decide your problems are your own. You do not blame them on your mother, the ecology, or the president. You realize you are in control of your own destiny.

Epictetus rightly said, "God has entrusted me with myself."

Accepting responsibility includes:

1. Believing that God has created you with freedom of choice in your everyday life.

2. Accepting that you are responsible for your thoughts, feelings, behavior, and choices.

3. Accepting the fact that you have made a commitment to obey Christ because you love Him (John 14:15), which means being responsible for your own spiritual growth.

4. Refusing to blame others for your mistakes and choices.

5. Removing the belief that others are responsible for where you are in your Christian walk.

6. Refusing to make excuses for failing to take responsibility or being proficient in a responsibility.

7. Refusing to point a finger at some past event in your life and trying to exempt yourself from a responsibility.

8. Making a specific plan for fulfilling a responsibility. It is TAR: Thoughts, Actions, and Results.

9. Renewing the mind daily by God's word, which means to accept the responsibilities He has assigned us (Romans 12:1–2).

10. Allowing others to take charge of their own responsibilities.

11. Refusing responsibilities because you don't feel qualified. Get qualified.

12. Being honest with yourself and making changes neces-
sary to become a more responsible Christian.

Responsibility Requires Accountability

When a teacher tells the class, "You are responsible for
reading chapters 10 and 11," and the students know there will
never be a test or discussion of the chapters, they won't read
or take seriously the teacher's assignments. In order for responsibility to work effectively, there must be accountability.

God is the God of accountability. He has not given us sug-
gestions so we may decide what we will and will not do. The
church is not a cafeteria where you pick and choose what you
will and will not do. The church is an army under orders from
the Commander-in-Chief to "fight the good fight of faith"
(1 Timothy 6:12; cf. 2 Timothy 2:1–3; 4:7).

Notice the following truths about accountability that relate to responsibility:

1. *There is going to be a judgment:* "It is appointed for men
to die once, but after this the judgment" (Hebrews 9:27).

2. *Every person shall give an account of himself:* "For we
shall all stand before the judgment seat of Christ. For it
is written: 'As I live, says the Lord, every knee shall bow
to Me, and every tongue shall confess to God.' So then
each of us shall give account of himself to God." (Romans
14:10–12). We can't secure someone to represent us or
plead our case.

3. *Each person in the judgment will give an account of the
deeds done in his or her body; not the deeds of someone
else:* "For we must all appear before the judgment seat of
Christ, that each may receive the things done in the body,
according to what he has done, whether good or bad"
(2 Corinthians 5:10).

4. *Each person in the judgment will give an account for all
the words he or she has spoken:* "But I say to you that for

every idle word men may speak, they will give account of in the day of judgment. For by your words you will be justified, and by your words you will be condemned" (Matthew 12:36–37).

5. *Accountability relates to stewardship faithfulness:* "So he called him and said to him, 'What is this I hear about you? Give an account of your stewardship, for you can no longer be steward'" (Luke 16:2).

6. *We receive the rewards of the deeds (actions) we do in our lives:* "And we indeed justly, for we receive the due rewards of our deeds; but this Man has done nothing wrong" (Luke 23:41). Even a thief on a cross knew the law of accountability.

As noted earlier in our study, Jesus inspected His churches and held them accountable for their responsibilities (actions). "Indeed I will cast her into a sickbed, and those who commit adultery with her into great tribulation, unless they repent of their deeds" (Revelation 2:22; cf. Matthew 7:21–23).

Regardless of whether we believe it or not, care or not, we all have an appointment with Christ, the Judge. We are not left to guess relative to what the standard of judgment will be. It will be the word of God:

> And if anyone hears My words and does not believe, I do not judge him; for I did not come to judge the world but to save the world. He who rejects Me, and does not receive My words, has that which judges him—the word that I have spoken will judge him in the last day (John 12:47–48).

The boss called in a new salesman and chewed him out for not emptying the trash can in his sales cubical. The salesman pleaded innocent because he didn't know that was one of his responsibilities as a salesman. He hadn't finished reading his new employee manual. He got a second chance. We will not get a second change to plead our case for not acting responsibly to the assignments God has given us. The good news is, He is giving us time to grow into maturity so we can accept and be more responsible (Hebrews 5:12). This is not to advocate ignorance or dragging our feet (Acts 17:30–31) but to remind us of God's graciousness as we grow from spiritual infancy to maturity in Christ.

We need to wake up to our personal spiritual responsibilities in Christ, remembering we are all headed to a day of accounting.

For Thought and Discussion

1. Why is there such a negative attitude toward responsibility?

2. As a child how did you learn about responsibility?

3. How has the clergy-laity concept impacted responsibility in the church? (We hear, for example, someone say, "That's the preacher's job!")

4. Why do so many Christians neglect their responsibilities?

5. Why has God always taught and enforced responsibility?

6. How does accountability relate to responsibility?

7. What is your most difficult responsibility as a Christian? Why?

8. What are some ways some try to avoid their responsibilities?

9. What additional observations do you have about this lesson?

10. How do you plan to use this lesson in your life? In the church?

13

Wake Up:
It's Time to Pursue Our Mission

Almost two thousand years ago Jesus Christ was taken outside Jerusalem and crucified as a common criminal. Early on the first day of the week His tomb was empty; He was proven to be the Son of God by His resurrection (cf. Romans 1:3–5). Sadly, today most of the world has not heard the Good News of the Savior's death, burial, and resurrection. This is in spite of the fact that He commanded His followers, then and now, to go and preach the gospel to every nation.

We sing these verses . . .

> "Lead me to some soul today"
> "Send the light"
> "Where He leads me I will follow"
> "I'll go where You want me to go"
> "Throw out the lifeline"

. . . and then place the song book back in the rack with little or no thought as to what we have just proclaimed. This raises the question: Why do we sing such songs about evangelism and then fail to do anything about reaching the lost? The apostle Paul taught that we must sing with the spirit, and sing with understanding (1 Corinthians 14:15). How does this apply to such verses as we have noted above? Paul also taught that in singing we teach and admonish one another (Ephesians 5:19; Colossians 3:16). Yet the evidence is that we don't follow through on what we are teaching each other in songs, hymns, and spiritual songs. This is a wake-up moment! Could it be that we need to be reminded by Jesus that we will give an account of every idle word we speak? (Matthew 12:36).

These verses are from some of my favorite hymns. They have been sung thousands of times through the years in countless churches. Yet I wonder how many singers of these grand old hymns have truly meant and applied the words to their personal lives and responsibilities assigned to them by God to share the gospel?

The alarm is ringing loudly and clearly trying to wake us to our responsibilities to be obedient to God's will for our lives. Jesus said, "If you love Me, keep My commandments" (John 14:15). Paul said, "Woe is me, if I do not preach the gospel!" (1 Corinthians 9:16). Do we have the same commitment? Do we dare say, *Go* is me?

God Places a Priority on Obedience

It has been said by an unknown person, that obedience, obey, and other related words are vulgar in our twenty-first century, as people have an aversion to obeying anything or anyone. A tenth grader stomps his foot and shouts at the teacher, "Nobody tells me what to do!" In like manner, believe it or not, there are some Christians, so-called, who will not let God tell them what to do. This is evidenced by the negligence in so many Christians' lives to assume the responsibilities given them by God.

The lingering question is, why do so many Christians fail, refuse, or neglect obedience to God's commands? One reason is that many have confused the rituals of Christianity with the responsibilities of Christianity. They see attending worship services as an end within itself, rather than a means of equipping them for fulfilling spiritual responsibilities. God is more interested in obedience than He is in ritual. Here is what Samuel told King Saul:

> Has the Lord as great delight in burnt offerings and sacrifices, as in obeying the voice of the Lord? Behold, to obey is better than sacrifice, and to heed than the fat of rams. For rebellion is as the sin of witchcraft, and stubbornness is as iniquity and idolatry. Because you have rejected the word of the Lord, He also has rejected you from being king (1 Samuel 15:22–23).

Yes, God commanded sacrifices of the Jews, just as He has commanded that we worship Him in spirit and in truth. So to think that mere outward compliance is all He wants misses the point of obedience from the inside out. The Pharisees were classic examples of outward show, but inwardly their hearts weren't committed to God's will (Matthew 23).

Here is another verse from a song: "Trust and obey, for there is no other way . . . "

Direction of Mission

In the midst of a city bus ride, a lady jumped up from her seat and asked the driver in a loud voice, "Where is this bus going?" The driver replied, "Fifth and Market!" The lady shouted back, "Stop this bus. I'm going in the wrong direction! I need to get off."

Most of us have had the experience of discovering we were going in the wrong direction. Direction is important in every area of life. Solomon wrote, "There is a way that seems right to a man, but its end is the way of death" (Proverbs 14:12).

We are where we are today because of the direction we have been traveling—right or wrong. Where we will be tomorrow depends on the course we start and follow today.

Christians need to wake up to the mission of the church. The bride of Christ is not on earth to entertain, make people feel better through self-help mantras, fill pockets with money, or create a self-pleasing environment. The church is on a rescue mission to snatch people out of the fire, build faith in the rescued, and send them back into the world on a rescue mission. Eternity is about more than pleasing God for one hour on Sunday morning, dropping a few bucks in a plate, and eating a tiny piece of bread. We are in a battle in which the flesh is fighting against the Spirit (Galatians 5:15–26).

Through the years preachers and teachers in the church have tried to present the mission of the church in practical, understandable, and workable terms, yet some still have a narrow or limited concept of the mission by Christ to His church. While there are many subsets we may use to define the mission of the church, I think it can be clearly defined by one word: evangelism. All subsets such as edification and equipping can be placed under one heading: evangelism.

How successful do you think an army, company, team, business, or club would be if none of these understood their basic mission? How about the church? How successful, from Christ's viewpoint, can a church be if it doesn't know, understand, and practice His mission? Let's spend a few minutes studying the major mission God has given the church, a mission we must be awake to and pursuing.

A Closer Look at Evangelism

My dear and late friend Clayton Pepper, editor of *Church Growth Magazine*, said, "Evangelism is the last thing we do and it's the first thing we give up." In over 45 years of full-time ministry I am saddened to say my observations agree with Clayton. Few congregations are obeying the Great Commission with any fervor in their communities. Many are dying because no new members are being added to the church.

A few years ago I visited a congregation that was using the baptistry as a storage place. Obviously they weren't expecting anyone to be baptized. An elder said if there was a baptism they would use the baptistry of a congregation across town.

Christians, wake up! The world is lost and we have been commanded to preach the gospel to every creature (Mark 16:15–16). There are no shortcuts or substitutes to accomplish God's mission for the church. The seed must be planted in good, honest, and patient hearts (Luke 8:11–16). Once a heart is pricked by the gospel, a set of human hands must lower the sinner into the waters of baptism (Acts 2:37–47). This requires going.

Many congregations give lip service to the Great Commission but in reality they practice the Great Omission. Outsiders are not reached and those who are obedient to the gospel are children of church members or a long-time attending spouse.

In my years of preaching I have seen one attempt after another, one gimmick after another, and one sure-fire approach after another used in efforts to reach the lost. We are on a continual search for an easy, non-threatening way to share the gospel. Programs come and go; classes are revived and classes die; the lost are still lost. The search goes on. To our shame, we go to the denominational scrap piles and drag out their thrown-away programs, believing they will halt our death march, but they don't. When will we learn to develop our own approaches in our indigenous soil?

We sing "Lead Me to Some Soul Today" in worship, and on our way home we drive by scores of lost souls; some are our neighbors and friends. We send missionaries to other countries, and even go and do campaign work in other countries, but don't lift a finger to share the gospel at work or with our neighbors and friends. How foreign this is to what we see in the early church.

Sow Your Own Seed

Christians, wake up! It is every member's responsibility to share the Good News as he is going in his world (Matthew 28:18–20). You can't any more hire a professional to sow your seed for you than you can hire someone to breathe for you.

Why aren't we obeying the Great Commission? Surveys say there may be several reasons:

1. *Perhaps we don't believe the lost are really lost, and if they are it's not all that bad.* We have poured cold water on the Bible doctrine of hell as punishment for lost sinners. Jesus asked some soul-searching questions in Mark 8:36–38 related to the value of a soul.

2. *Perhaps it is because of a failure to take seriously the priority Jesus gave to evangelism in the Great Commission.* Here are five portions of Scripture revealing His emphasis on sharing the gospel:

   - Matthew 28:19–20—Go make disciples of all nations.
   - Mark 16:15—Go into all the world and preach the good news to all creation.
   - Luke 24:47—And repentance and forgiveness of sins will be preached in His name to all nations.
   - John 20:21—As the Father has sent Me, I am sending you.
   - Acts 1:8—And you will be My witnesses in Jerusa-

lem, and in all Judea and Samaria, and to the ends of the earth.

3. *In some congregations the sharing of the gospel has been neglected or given only lip service because the emphasis has been turned inward.* Housekeeping is a priority. Busyness is an end within itself. Programs! The end in mind seems to be bigger and better programs, none of which are converting sinners from the errors of their ways.

4. *Our concept of God has a direct impact on how we respond to the command to share the gospel.* Failing to see Him high, holy, and lifted up won't bring the response it did in Isaiah's life when he saw the glory of God (Isaiah 6:1–8). When God wanted to know who would go for Him, Isaiah replied, "Here am I! Send me."

5. *Motivation is another major reason many are failing to share the gospel.* Faith in God and His word are the two powers that generate motivation to obey God. This is why "without faith it is impossible to please Him" (Hebrews 11:6). If we truly believe God is who He claims to be (cf. John 17:3) and He will do what He has promised to do, we will be about our Father's business (Luke 2:48–52).

6. *Many Christians seem to have good intentions relative to sharing the gospel, but they keep procrastinating.* Jesus addressed this mentality: "Do you not say, 'There are still four months and then comes the harvest'? Behold, I say to you, lift up your eyes and look at the fields, for they are already white for harvest" (John 4:35). You can't see the harvest field while sitting in the comfort of a padded pew. The harvest—lost souls—are out in the field where you must sow the seed (cf. Luke 8:11–17); it is where you must go.

7. *A frequent and common reason Christians fail to share the gospel is fear.* They don't want to lose friends or make associates angry. It is as though they are ashamed of the very gospel that saved them (Romans 1:14–16). It is not cool to be a politically incorrect person. Oh, someday they

will get up the courage when the time is right. Sadly, many look into the casket of those with whom they planned to share the gospel, but they waited too long.

8. *Many isms—liberalism, cynicism, narcissism, skepticism, pluralism, secularism, and privatism—have sidetracked Christians relative to sharing the gospel.* They have too much of the world in them to convert the world. It would mean they would have to change.

9. *Numerous other excuses stand in the way of many who aren't planning to share the gospel:*

   - "Evangelism is not my gift."
   - "I am waiting for an easy evangelism approach."
   - "I don't know enough."
   - "Our church has many problems; I don't want to bring anyone into the confusion. We need a clean house."

It's sad to say, but a deliberate disobedience to the command to share the gospel with the lost is a major reason why the gospel is not being taught. Somehow many think they are exempt from the command to "preach the gospel." That isn't true.

The Gospel Has Been High-Jacked

In the first century the apostle Paul warned the Galatians against perverting the gospel:

> I marvel that you are turning away so soon from Him who called you in the grace of Christ, to a different gospel, which is not another; but there are some who trouble you and want to pervert the gospel of Christ (Galatians 1:6–7).

Self-Evaluation

Take a few minutes and evaluate where you are at this time in your spiritual journey relative to sharing the gospel with the lost:

1. ____Yes ____No   I have shared the gospel in the past month.

2. ___Yes ___No I have shared the gospel in the past three months.

3. ___Yes ___No I have shared the gospel in the past six months.

4. ___Yes ___No I have shared the gospel in the past twelve months.

5. ___Yes ___No I have never shared the gospel

Congregational Evaluation

Take a few minutes and evaluate where your congregation is relative to sharing the gospel:

_____ Number of baptisms in past 12 months.

_____ Number of baptisms is past 24 months.

_____ Number of baptisms in past 36 months.

Emphasis on Evangelism

During the past twelve months, using a scale of 1 (1 percent) to 100 (100 percent), how much emphasis has been given to evangelism in your congregation in the following categories?

_____ In the sermons

_____ In the Bible classes

_____ In special lectureships or workshops

_____ In campaigns and outreach efforts

_____ In small group discussions

_____ In bulletin articles

_____ In congregational prayer

For Thought and Discussion

1. Why should we evangelize?

2. Why is evangelism so urgent?

3. Why is evangelism neglected?

4. How can we become more evangelistic?

5. What is your greatest challenge in sharing the gospel?

6. How does Luke 13:3, 5 relate to evangelism?

7. How does 2 Corinthians 5:14 relate to evangelism?

8. What one intentional thing are you going to do because of this lesson?